Dennis Kemp

Nine Years at the Gold Coast

Dennis Kemp

Nine Years at the Gold Coast

ISBN/EAN: 9783743313620

Manufactured in Europe, USA, Canada, Australia, Japa

Cover: Foto ©ninafisch / pixelio.de

Manufactured and distributed by brebook publishing software (www.brebook.com)

Dennis Kemp

Nine Years at the Gold Coast

NINE YEARS

AT

THE GOLD COAST

BY THE

REV. DENNIS KEMP

LATE GENERAL SUPERINTENDENT WESLEYAN MISSIONS
GOLD COAST DISTRICT

London

MACMILLAN AND CO. Limited

NEW YORK: THE MACMILLAN COMPANY

1898

All rights reserved

RICHARD CLAY AND SONS, LIMITED,
LONDON AND BUNGAY.

TO

MY WIFE

PREFACE

THE considerations which induced me to yield to the wishes of personal friends to attempt a description of mission work at the Gold Coast were :—

First, a desire to furnish the supporters of our Missionary Society with such information as might not merely be of interest, but which would, to a certain extent, give the *results* of missionary enterprise in a small but important part of the foreign field. Hitherto our friends have been under the necessity of deriving their information from travellers whose literary talents have been out of all proportion to their opportunities for studying the subject of missions.

Secondly, I have entertained the hope that it might be possible to give such information as would be useful to young men in training for work abroad. I have endeavoured to show that each of the colleagues with whom I have had the pleasure and privilege of being associated has contributed towards the growth of the Gold Coast Mission. It is hoped that future missionaries will thus learn that there is ample scope for the exercise of a great variety of gifts on the foreign field.

And then, as experience has taught me that there is a growing interest in this old British possession, I have ventured to touch upon topics other than those of a purely missionary character.

In the presence of the literary critic I exceedingly fear and quake, and tremblingly plead "guilty," and urge "extenuating circumstances" to every conceivable and inconceivable charge that may be brought against me from a purely literary point of view. I am well aware that much more might have been written, even by so incompetent a pen as my own, but to have attempted a larger work would have required more time from my present ministerial duties than I feel warranted in taking.

The reader will doubtless observe that I have had little occasion to make use of materials furnished by previous writers on West Africa; in mentioning the early connection of the Portuguese with the Gold Coast I have, however, placed myself under an obligation to Mr. C. P. Lucas' "Historical Geography of West Africa" (Clarendon Press), and in referring to the trade relations of the Colony I have made use of Mr. Hesketh Bell's address to the Liverpool Chamber of Commerce. I sincerely regret the fact that it was only after finally leaving Africa that I mustered sufficient courage to record my experience. Fortunately my Gold Coast letters to my mother have been preserved; these, naturally, have been indispensable to me. Articles and photographs by myself which have appeared in our missionary magazine, *Work and Workers*, have been placed at my disposal by the Editor. My old colleagues, the Reverends S. C. Hall and J. S. Ellenberger, have also furnished me with information, for which I am most grateful.

I hesitate to associate the name of the Reverend W. T. A. Barber, M.A., B.D., with the reading of the proof sheets. If I take the liberty I must explain that my friend's considerate regard for the susceptibilities of an inexperienced author has considerably restrained him, or he might have "corrected" my work beyond all hope of recognition.

ELIAMA, ST. URSULA GROVE,
    SOUTHSEA, *March 3rd*, 1898.

CONTENTS

CHAPTER I

Offer of services for the Gold Coast Mission—Particulars as to outfit, &c.—Notes of introduction to friends in Africa . . *Pages* 1—7

CHAPTER II

Furnishes brief information respecting the various tribes of the Gold Coast—Our early relations with them, and the value of their country commercially—Concluding with remarks respecting the Fetish religion . . . . *Pages* 8—26

CHAPTER III

Contains a revelation to the Author, the study of which proves that the Missionary's preconceived ideas respecting his vocation did not harmonise with his actual experience—Suggestions are also respectfully offered to the aspiring West African resident in reference to the preservation of health, and the reader is introduced to an invaluable colleague . . . . *Pages* 27—47

CHAPTER IV

Deals with the difficulties in introducing Christian ideas respecting marriage.—Reflections concerning the character of the native, and references to our school at Cape Coast . . . . . . *Pages* 48—67

CHAPTER V

Gives an account of a journey into the "Bush," with glimpses of forest scenery, and an introduction to the rural members of the Church . . . . *Pages* 68—85

CONTENTS

CHAPTER VI

Relates circumstances which will summon an immense concourse of people—a funeral, a fire, or a festival—And has a reference to Elmina Castle and its connection with the Ashanti War of 1873—And concludes with remarks respecting personal associates
Pages 86—98

CHAPTER VII

The arrival of the Roman Catholic Missionaries at Cape Coast—Theological differences do not affect personal friendships—The Reverend T. J. Price and his difficulties with the vernacular—His Excellency Sir W. Brandford Griffith, K.C.M.G.—Happy relations with Anglican Clergy. . . . . *Pages* 99—111

CHAPTER VIII

Records a memorable journey through Aburah and Assin—And furnishes illustrations of the Fetish priestcraft . . *Pages* 112—133

CHAPTER IX

The first serious break in the European Staff—A journey to the gold mines—Extracts from Reports—Peacemaking between converts—Advantages of African workers among Africans—The arrival of the Reverend A. W. Hall—Industrial training—Commercial interests in West Africa not essentially selfish . . . *Pages* 134—151

CHAPTER X

The Missionary is joined by his wife—The urgent need of lady workers in Africa—Suggestions respecting the sanitation of the Colony—A journey to the Aburi sanatorium, and an account of the Croboe heathen customs . . . . *Pages* 152—168

CHAPTER XI

The Drink Traffic—Our attitude as a Church towards the question—Suggestions to the Government—Reckless travelling—His Excellency the Governor and the Colonial Secretary testify to the value of Mission work—Proposal to establish Girls' Boarding School at Aburi—Practical support of the Home Government
Pages 169—191

CHAPTER XII

The steamship "Calabar"—Advance in shipping accommodation—Difficulties in negotiating land questions with the unsophisticated African — A plague of locusts — "Liberty, Fraternity Equality"—The Gold Coast Board of Education—Difficulties in building—The transport question—Kru boys to the rescue
Pages 192—209

CHAPTER XIII

Improved locomotion in our journeying—The arrival of Miss A. I. Jackman, and her lamented death—Miss Mary H. Kingsley—Missionary methods and Missionary converts and their critics—The devotion of Basle Missionaries—An illustration of the power of the Gospel. . . . . *Pages* 210—229

CHAPTER XIV

The British occupation of Ashanti—A respectful tribute to the British Army and Navy as agents that make for justice and mercy—An account of a journey to Kumasi . . . . *Pages* 230—264

CHAPTER XV

The last voyage to the Coast, in company with kindred spirits—A brief summary of Mission work, and references to three "Missionary-made men" . . . . *Pages* 265—276

LIST OF ILLUSTRATIONS

	To face page
Map of the Gold Coast Colony . . . . *Frontispiece*	
View of Cape Coast.	6
Market Place, Cape Coast.	16
A Native Goldsmith	16
Types of Native Beauty.	16
Emerging from the Forest (photo. by Rev. D. Hinchcliff) . . .	20
Cape Coast Castle and West Indian Soldiers	28
The Tender Care of Fanti Boatmen	28
Interior of Wesley Church, Cape Coast (photo. by Rev. D. Hinchcliff)	32
A Neat Head-dress.	50
Preparing a Meal	50
Native Goldsmiths' Work.	56
Ga Chief's Gold Breast Ornaments	56
Gold Coast Matrons and Children	61
Types of Native Dress	80
The late Sir W. Brandford Griffith, K.C.M.G.	108
Fetishes.	124
Fetishes.	128
Essaman Gold Mines (photo. by Rev. J. T. F. Halligey) . . .	136
Tree Bridge, River Whin (photo. by Rev. J. T. F. Halligey . .	136
Elmina Castle	150
Young Carpenters' Work (Industrial Education)	150
Beach at Axim, with Mahogany Logs	160
Palaver at Akropong, Houssa Soldiers "At Ease"	164

LIST OF ILLUSTRATIONS

To face page

A Faithful Friend in the Hour of Sickness (photo. by Rev. J. T. F. Halligey)	186
Miss Ellenberger. Aburi Girls' School (photo. by Rev. D. Hinchcliff)	204
Specimens of School Girls' Dress	204
Grand Bassa Labourers	210
A Halt in the Forest	210
Natives of Akwapim (photo. by Rev. D. Hinchcliff)	222
Hotel Accommodation (photo. by Rev. D. Hinchcliff)	226
Akim Executioner, and Stool Carrier	232
Preparing to Start	236
A Fanti Bush Village	236
Hillside Scenery (photo. by Rev. D. Hinchcliff)	242
An Emancipated Slave (photo. by Rev. D. Hinchcliff)	242
Ashanti Gold Weights	248
A Gold Coast Chief and Visitors	248
King Prempeh and Suite at Elmina Castle	257
Curiosities from the Gold Coast	272

NINE YEARS AT THE GOLD COAST

CHAPTER I

OFFER OF SERVICES FOR THE GOLD COAST MISSION—PARTICULARS AS TO OUTFIT, ETC.—NOTES OF INTRODUCTION TO FRIENDS IN AFRICA

IT was in the early part of 1887 that my attention was seriously drawn to the Gold Coast. I use the word serious advisedly: for, with the prospect of missionary life before me, I was naturally interested in all missionary work; and when it was reported that three men, *i.e.*, half of our force at the Gambia and the Gold Coast, had died within six months, I naturally became *very serious*, and promptly decided that West Africa was *the* part of the world all prudent men should avoid. A few months later, however, when volunteers from Handsworth College were invited to fill one of the vacancies, a resistless fascination seized me, which I have never been able to shake off; and, with the consent of my friends, my services were offered and accepted, subject to a satisfactory report as to physical fitness from the medical officer, Dr., now Sir, C. Gage Brown.

There always was, and I suppose always will be, a certain amount of sentiment about the volunteers for missionary work in West Africa. There was sentiment in my offer—though that sentiment has long since faded away, and it is now regarded as a very real sacrifice *not* to be able to continue in that interesting part of the world. And yet, in common with other missionaries, I never for one moment entertained the idea of leaving my bones in Africa : I went simply hoping and expecting to be of use. And now I have to record my devout thankfulness to Almighty God for the health and strength that have enabled me to take part in that work. May I repeat a sentence or two from my early notes ? "The essential qualifications of the volunteer for mission work in West Africa are (1) a deep abiding conviction that one has chosen the path of duty ; (2) a good physical constitution ; (3) the exercise of the greatest possible prudence, the absence of fear, and implicit confidence in God."

My first care after securing the necessary medical certificate was to prepare my outfit. As this may be of interest to the reader, I may as well give a general idea of the same, omitting any reference to the needless and expensive items with which I burdened myself, mentioning only that which is likely to be of service to any one contemplating a term of eighteen months' residence at the Gold

Coast. In making up the outfit list the ordinary light summer clothing may well form the basis of calculation. Thicker clothing will only be of service during the cold voyage to Grand Canary, and through the Trade winds—so treacherous on the return voyage. Eighteen months of a West African humid atmosphere, together with well-known, though scarcely approved, methods of the native laundryman, will be quite equal to three years of wear and tear in England. Flannel or merino should always be worn next the skin. A good helmet and white cotton umbrella are, of course, indispensable—lighter hats may be worn late in the afternoon. Inclination has often led one to wear the loosest and lightest clothing. But it must be borne in mind that the "tailor makes the man" in the coast towns of Africa, as well as in England. In preparing for the rainy season it may be worth while to say that as much rain falls in a day at the Gold Coast as falls in Manchester in a rather wet month. And what more need one say?—except that care must be taken that the waterproof cloak is *stitched*, or it may, as mine has done, fall to pieces. Due care must be given to the requisites of bed-covering. Blankets are necessary, particularly in the wet season, and in case of fever. Pyjamas are invariably worn; and the flannel belt, which I have found of great service in warding off dysentery. Sponges, bath-towels, etc., will suggest themselves. Ironware for the kitchen, hardware, plate and cutlery for personal use must be furnished. In ordering these bear in mind that visitors drop in occasionally. In our free and easy life we have sometimes borrowed from the traveller: but it may chance that although your servant has been unusually skilful in breaking your ware, your visitor will not have the necessary articles on his person, so that it is well to be provided with at least a change. Do not forget the table linen: a neatly arranged table helps to tempt the appetite, which is often fastidious. In travelling take enamelled ironware: not that it is pleasanter to use, but your cook sometimes "forgets" to see that the table requisites are safely packed; and your carrier, after resting on the travelling-case, is greatly surprised to find a general smash, and you feel—well, you may fill in the rest as your fancy dictates. Whatever else is overlooked take care to provide yourself with a good filter. "Maignens" are the most serviceable I have had in use. It is well to be supplied with provisions from England. The number of houses engaged in this particular trade is legion. Crosse and Blackwell are always most obliging in executing orders. The local stores do not keep the greatest variety, and for other reasons it has been found an advantage to import direct. Chlorodyne, anti-febrin, and quinine should be kept in every home. Antibilious compounds are worth, in my judgment, *two* "guineas a box."

Books are needed in Africa as much as in England. But they suffer from the damp air—covers come to grief in a very short time. Cockroaches and white ants "inwardly digest," even though they do not "read, mark, and learn," the contents. A few inexpensive knick-knacks help to make a great contrast to the bare walls of some quarters one has visited.

And now, having sent the heavy luggage to the agents, Messrs. Elder, Dempster & Co. at Liverpool, three days previously, labelled "wanted" or "not wanted on the voyage," as the case may be, it is possible to take the light luggage as late as the midnight train on any Friday from Euston, and, after breakfast in the neighbourhood of Lime Street, to find our way to the Prince's landing-stage in comfortable time for the tender which is to leave at 10 o'clock to take us to one of the "African" or the "British and African" companies' vessels. We must not raise our expectations too high. Our vessel is neither an Atlantic liner, a P. and O., nor a Cape boat. But the line is being made increasingly comfortable; and, with the very genial captains, it is possible to have an exceedingly pleasant voyage, as far as the companies are concerned. I must emphasise the last sentence, for my first voyage was *not* pleasant. We had *weather!* "And what could have been expected with *three parsons* aboard?" exclaimed the men "forrud." No; I think I must defer a description of a voyage until a more favourable opportunity presents itself. For several days

I sympathised with our Irish surgeon, who assured me that he was "sorrah that he had a stomach at ahl." And then our companions were not of the most select. One, a lady of the theatrical profession, who left us at Grand Canary, has lately been compelled to release her husband from his matrimonial vow. Another, a gentleman, has since died, leaving *two* wives and families in England to mourn his loss. And a third, a few years ago, was sentenced to two years' imprisonment for embezzlement.

I find on referring to notes of that time that my worthy chief, the Reverend J. T. F. Halligey, was on the voyage most thoughtful and kind. And my friend, Bryan Roe, who was returning to Lagos, was just the cheerful companion that many in this country would expect him to be. One incident must be mentioned: on the 16th of December a concert was given by artistes, who, according to the programme, "had come a long distance." The entertainment was greatly appreciated by a company of about thirty, who contributed very handsomely to seamen's institutions.

I was not able to leave a message, as desired, with friends at Gibraltar, for the very reason that I was not able to take notes of introduction to the Cape. A voyage from Cape Coast to the Cape of Good Hope is a thousand miles further than is the voyage from England to the Cape! I found that the worthy missionary secretary, who imagined that a missionary who preached at Bathurst in the morning might

CAPE COAST.

preach at Free Town, Sierra Leone, in the evening, was not aware that the two places were five hundred miles apart. We have had occasion to inform a most successful English schoolmaster that Bathurst was not merely *one*, but nearly one thousand five hundred miles from Cape Coast. My experience of West Africa has made me exceedingly cautious in asking questions concerning the geography of any part of the world. I may add that my new home, I found, was 1° 10′ west longitude, and 5° 6′ latitude north of the Equator.

CHAPTER II

FURNISHES BRIEF INFORMATION RESPECTING THE VARIOUS TRIBES OF THE GOLD COAST; OUR EARLY RELATIONS WITH THEM, AND THE VALUE OF THEIR COUNTRY COMMERCIALLY—CONCLUDING WITH REMARKS RESPECTING THE FETISH RELIGION

As we have agreed to defer for a time the description of a voyage, it may be convenient to introduce a few paragraphs respecting the various tribes of the Gold Coast and Hinterland, referring the reader for detailed particulars to the list of authors who have dealt with the subject at great length. I must honestly confess that when I first embarked for Africa I knew as little of the history of the Fantis as of the mythical personage who is said to reside in the lunar regions. Constant and prominent references to Ashantis and Fantis naturally lead to the conclusion that these two tribes alone represent this part of West Africa. A reference to our map will at once indicate the erroneousness of this supposition.

I am indebted to notes by my native colleague, the Reverend J. B. Anaman, F.R.G.S., for the particulars here furnished respecting his fellow-countrymen. Most of the tribes inhabiting the Gold Coast originally lived in Central Africa, from which districts they were driven towards the coast by Moslem propagandists who invaded their territory in order to win them to that faith. Some of the emigrants, notably the Ashantis,[1] and their near kinsmen, the Fantis, settled in the regions of the Kong mountains, in the district then called by the Arabs Wangara. The city built by the Fantis was Takyiman, from which in time, being hard pressed by the Ashantis, they withdrew southward, till gradually they overspread the whole region now known as Fanti-land.

The great language of the emigrants was Akan, which is spoken by the peoples inhabiting the Gold Coast and Ashanti, thus marking the common origin of the tribes. The most important dialect of the Akan language is Fanti, which is generally understood throughout the Gold Coast, but is chiefly spoken by the Fantis, Elminas, and Chamas. The Accras and Adanme-speaking tribes are believed to have been closely related, as well as the Ahantas, Apollonians, Sehwis, and Aowins. These tribes were comprehended in seven great families, in which the members still class themselves and recognise each other, without regard to national distinctions, viz.—

1. Nsonna, Dwimina, etc.

---

[1] It is suggested that the prevalence of a severe famine led to the adoption of the names Asuan-tsi-fu, gatherers of asuan (a poisonous weed), and Fan-tsi-fu, gatherers of fan (a cabbage).

2. Annona, Yoko, Aguna, Eguana, etc.
3. Twidan, Eburotuw, etc.
4. Kwonna, Ebiradzi, Odumna, Dinyina, etc.
5. Aburadzi, Eduana, Ofurna, Egyirina, etc.
6. Intwa, Abadzi, etc.
7. Adwinadzi, Aowin, etc.

There are several branches of each family, known by different names in different localities. Confusion has arisen through the erroneous division by some writers of these branches into twelve families. This division is inexplicable to the natives, who have a tradition that mankind comprises seven great families or nations.

The effects of contact with the civilised world upon the natives have certainly been varied. It is believed that before they were driven from their old home they traded in articles of European manufacture through the Greeks of Alexandria. The linen of Egypt and the scarlet cloths of Carthage, together with the famous aggrey[1] beads, reached them through the Berbers. The linen is supposed to have been used by them, as at this day, for the purpose of indicating sanctity or festivity. Large umbrellas made of scarlet cloth were considered by them great embellishments of a state. Aggrey beads were worn as ornaments; and the wealth of an individual was estimated by the abundance of these,

---

[1] The aggrey beads are now exceedingly rare. They are supposed to have been made by the Phœnicians. Their commercial value is reckoned at double their weight in gold.

or the gold which he possessed. In very ancient times, gold, silver, ivory, apes and peacocks were the products of Central Africa. Some of these articles most probably formed part of the merchandise conveyed into the regions beyond the great Desert during these years.

In studying the early history of the peoples with whom we are dealing there is not the aid that is furnished in the history of other nations, by ancient inscriptions, architectural monuments, or sepulchral remains. Until quite recently no attempt was made to reduce their language to writing; and materials used in the erection of buildings were of such a nature that they have long since amalgamated with the earth, as, indeed, is the case with towns which were quite famous twenty-five years ago. No real help is afforded by the early enterprise of navigating nations, for the difficulties and currents of the West African coast proved a greater barrier to progress than does the treacherous climate of to-day.

Very reluctantly, therefore, we must confess that we have no definite information of any extensive trade with the coast until towards the close of the fifteenth century. French writers, indeed, have claimed for their fellow-countrymen the honour of discovering, or rather of re-discovering, the Gold Coast in 1364, and it is supposed that a fort was built by the travellers at Elmina in 1382. But the trade relations if any must have been unsatisfactory, for they withdrew altogether a few years before the Portuguese, encouraged and stimulated by the example of their brave and noble-minded Prince Henry the Navigator, first landed at Elmina in 1465.

On "August 12th, 1553, there sailed from Portsmouth two goodly ships, the *Primrose*, and the *Lyon*, with a pinnace called the *Moon*, and seven score lusty men, under two expert pilots and politick Captains; to one whereof the King of Portugal had committed the custody of Guinney against the French; happy was that man that could go with them. . . .

"They brought from thence at this Voyage, four hundred pound weight and odd of Gold, of two and twenty carrats, and one grain in fineness; also six and thirty Buts of grains, and about two-hundred and fifty Elephant's Teeth of all quantities. . . . Some of them were as big as a man's thigh above the knee, and weighed about fourscore and ten pound weight a peece. . . . These great Teeth, or tusks, grow in the upper jaw downward, and not in the nether jaw upward, wherein the Painters and Arras-workers are deceived."

The voyage truly was remarkable. "Part of such Flesh as they carried with them out of England, which putrified there, *became sweet again* at their return to the clime of temperate Regions." And stranger still: "Here is a Tree called the Oyster-Tree, that bears oysters three times in the year; but I beleeve it hath been since Noah's flood when the fish forgot their way into the sea again."[1]

At various times the French, Portuguese, Dutch, Danes and Germans have settled for long or short periods at the Gold Coast. Indeed, until half a century since, the Dutch and the Danes as well as the English had forts at Accra, the present seat of Government. The last to retire from the Gold Coast and leave the English in sole possession were the Dutch, who transferred Elmina Castle to our Government in 1873.

I have said that difficulties of navigation have proved a barrier to progress in West Africa. A moment's reflection will suggest the possibility of a retrograde movement for the natives, during the three centuries that their land was open to the Christian nations of Europe. It must be borne in mind that, partly as a result of the slave traffic, in which this country took a prominent part, the natives of the Gold Coast were brought into constant communication with the very outcasts of European society. Buccaneers, pirates, outlaws and desperadoes of every description found their way to the Coast as they did to the West Indies and the Spanish main. Very naturally they took with them the most horrible vices that a human mind could conceive. And even in the early part of the present century English soldiers who had committed grave offences were offered the chance of existing in

[1] *The Golden Coast, or a Description of Guinney.* London, 1665.

West Africa, as the alternative to the gallows. What an awful influence must such as these have exerted upon the natives, who were already deeply degraded!

And what of the Gold Coast Government during the period mentioned? If we may accept the testimony of one who was an officer of the Government from 1834 to 1852, and who had access to the archives of the Castle, the members of those early councils were absolutely without feeling. To all outward appearance the native existed only in order to satisfy the greed of England's representatives. Until the abolition of slavery in 1807 not one single lasting benefit was conferred upon the people, and but few isolated advantages on individuals; while the magnitude of the curse inflicted upon the unhappy natives is simply beyond all words.

We have seen that the early visitors to the Coast were attracted by the wealth of the country; it may be worth while to devote a little space to the study of the present commercial value of the Colony to Great Britain.

The Colony possesses a seaboard of nearly 400 miles. There are nineteen ports of entry; the most important are Accra, the seat of Government, and Cape Coast. Dealing first with imports we find that the principal articles of trade are cotton, woollen and silk goods, spirits, hardware, coopers' stores, rice, flour, provisions, tobacco, building materials, and wearing apparel. The total value in

1895 amounted to £931,537. The United Kingdom contributed 67½ per cent., British Colonies 10, and foreign countries 22½ per cent. America and the Continent are responsible, as far as the native consumption is concerned, for the whole of the spirit traffic. Concerning the latter may I repeat, and emphasise, what I wrote four years ago? "The town of Cape Coast has a population of 15,000. I have no hesitation in saying that, on an average, not two instances arising out of drunkenness are tried by the District Commissioner in twelve months." I shall have occasion later on to refer to this liquor traffic.

The quality of the goods imported is generally of the commonest description. British manufacturers tell us that the very worst rubbish possible for machinery to "throw together" is very often made expressly for the West African market. The leading merchants keep superior goods, and encourage their sale; but, unfortunately, the demand is usually for the lowest priced article. In Cape Coast it is possible to obtain "an apology," at any rate, for almost everything that is made. Native tailors, good, bad, and indifferent, abound. There is also a very creditable attempt at boot-making.

Natives have as much regard for English provisions as for English dress. When we bear in mind the fact that to the original cost of provisions is added twenty-five per cent. for shipping expenses and custom-house charges, to say nothing of the necessarily heavy expenses incurred in retailing, it is amazing that so much is consumed. Aerated waters which are retailed in England at a shilling or eighteenpence a dozen, realise sixpence each at Cape Coast! At weddings they are disposed of by the score!

An enormous quantity of gunpowder is annually imported into the Colony, but, like the spirits, it spreads over a wide area. It is said that kings and chiefs can muster 100,000 warriors who possess Birmingham "gas-pipe flint-locks," which are much more dangerous to the owner than to the foe. Very little ammunition is used in actual warfare; but great quantities are consumed at funerals, weddings, palavers, and fetish ceremonies.

On any day in the week Mohammedans in their white gowns, with their wares, may be seen in the market-place seated on their mats or engaged with visitors from the Bush. From nine to eleven o'clock on every morning in the week a great crowd, composed chiefly of women and girls, contributes to a perfect Babel of noise. This business resort is provided by the Government principally for the convenience of the vendors of meat, fruit, and vegetables. In other parts of the town there are well-drained streets with extremely well-built business and residential houses on either side. In these respects Cape Coast and Accra are far in advance of other towns in the Colony.

And now a word or two with reference to exports.

MARKET PLACE, CAPE COAST.

CAPE COAST GOLDSMITH.

[To face page 16.

TYPES OF NATIVE BEAUTY.

The principal are palm oil, palm kernels, rubber, gold dust, mahogany, kola nuts, and monkey skins. It is gratifying to note that the new industries, coffee and cocoa cultivation, are being pushed forward. The total value of all exports for 1895 amounted to £877,803, of which 67 per cent. was shipped to England, 4 per cent. to British Colonies, and the remainder to foreign countries.

The mineral from which the Colony takes its name is not shipped in great quantities. But prior to the discovery of the Californian and Australian gold-fields, the principal supply of the precious metal was drawn from the West Coast of Africa, and especially from the Gold Coast. The Portuguese, the French, the Danes, the Dutch, and the English have drawn during the last four centuries not less than six hundred millions sterling! The Colony is still very rich in the mineral. I have met a miner, with considerable experience in South Africa, who gave it as his opinion that there were "twenty Johannesbergs at the Gold Coast." The statement was made in all seriousness. It is, of course, quite possible that my informant was mistaken, but we have nevertheless good reason to believe that the supply of gold is inexhaustible. The unhealthiness of the climate seriously interferes with the management of operations at the mines. It must be borne in mind that in the last century white traders and coloured chiefs could command the services of thousands of slaves. The small amount now shipped

C

is obtained principally from the five or six mining companies in the Wassaw district.

Some good samples of ivory are also shipped. I have seen a tusk which weighed ninety-six pounds —a sufficient load for two men to carry any considerable distance. The awful stories of Stanley and Cameron, of the destruction of human life and property in procuring this article, have no reference to Gold Coast exports. Elephants are found quite near the protectorate. It is needless to say that "slaves," in the ordinary acceptation of the term, are unknown in the Colony.

The Gold Coast ranks third among the rubber-producing countries of the world. In 1883 only twenty-five tons were shipped; in 1895 the amount was almost eighteen hundred tons, valued, in the Colony, at £322,070. The rubber is obtained principally from various species of Landolphia and the Urostigura Vogelii, which grow in abundance in Ashanti, Akim, and Krepi. The native method of collecting it reminds one of the fable of the old lady with the goose that laid the golden eggs.

Palm oil, which is extensively used in South Wales in the manufacture of tin plate, and in the fabrication of soap and candles (and margarine ?), is shipped in considerable quantities. Upwards of four million gallons were exported in 1895; at the same time, the kernels from the same tree, used in the manufacture of oil, amounted to fifteen thousand tons.

Valuable shipments of mahogany are sent to Europe every week. The quantity during the year varies according as the season is dry or wet. A dry season, of course, means low rivers, consequently inadequate facilities for floating the logs.

It may be mentioned that between 1881 and 1895 the imports and exports of the Colony have been trebled; and, with the settled state of affairs in Ashanti, there is every probability of the trade increasing considerably. When this fact is considered, it is worth while to give attention to the natives as consumers of our manufactures, and as contributors to our necessities.

No one supposes that the Government occupies the Gold Coast for purely philanthropic purposes. Were that indeed the case, we should be able to report very much greater progress than facts admit. Nevertheless, it is worthy of note that in recent years vast improvements have been made in the sanitation of the important towns, and that in these towns there are now hospitals and qualified surgeons. The Government encourages education, which is making enormous strides throughout the Colony. Law is administered as in England. Order is maintained by a strong police force, called the Gold Coast Constabulary. This force includes both a military and a civil police, the former branch being recruited from the Houssas, the latter from the natives of the Colony, under the direction of English officers. Communication between the principal towns of the coast, and also with Kumasi, is effected by telegraph, and the coast towns have the advantage of a land, as well as ocean, post. Civilisation in the towns thus benefited is further suggested by the presence of street lamps. Considerable attention is being given to road-making. The Legislative Council is composed of the Governor, the Colonial Secretary, the Attorney-General, the Treasurer, the Inspector-General of Police, the Chief Justice, and of two nominated unofficial members. It is said that there are never more than two dissentients to any measure introduced to the Council.

The natives are, of course, generally speaking, pagans. Their repugnance to Mohammedanism is not as great to-day as it was when they fled before the propagandists' sword; but one is surprised to note how little advance that religion makes with the natives of the Gold Coast. There is, it is true, an influx of Mohammedans; but this is due to the formation of an armed force of Houssas, natives of one of the Central Sudan States, situated about five hundred miles to the north-east of the Gold Coast.

Above and beyond the polytheism which everywhere prevails among the pagans, there is the acknowledgment of a Supreme Being who controls the affairs of the universe. The name given to this Being is Nyankupon (the Great Friend), otherwise Otcheranpon (the Never-Failing One); the literal idea being that of leaning against some stupendous

[*To face page* 20.

EMERGING FROM THE GLOOMY FOREST.

object which never yields—as the rock never yields from under the limpet.¹ But at the same time they acknowledge subordinate deities, who are supposed to reside in the angry sea; the swift running stream; the placid lake; the woody grove, awe-inspiring and majestic;² the bleak rock, capable, in a sense, of telling the story of the ages; also in objects the work of men's hands: to these they give their reverence. Again, they worship the spirits of the departed, together with the images which their priests consecrate for their homage, and in which the spirits of the dead are supposed to reside. There are deities for particular houses; others for a whole town, and others, again, for the nation at large.

From the great "Nyankupon" all good gifts descend; "in Him they live and move and have their being." And yet, curiously, no appeal is ever made to the Great Friend, for it is supposed that He allows the affairs of the universe to be ordered exclusively by the inimical agents whom it becomes necessary to constantly propitiate. Before the strong arm of the Government intervened the

---

[1] *Vide* address by the Reverend Mark C. Hayford, native missionary.

[2] "A dark impenetrable mystery seems to hang beneath the shade of the gloomy forest, and in some degree, at least, accounts for the idolatry and superstition of the indwellers. Instinctively the question presents itself, 'Where could rapine and man-stealing and murder be more securely performed? Where the cry of affliction and despair so easily stifled? Where could the human mind find a scene more calculated to impress it with a superstitious awe, or to prepare it for the bloody rites of the pagan worship, as this dark awe-giving forest?'"— *Eighteen Years on the Gold Coast.*

victims selected for sacrifice were invariably human, and were usually decapitated or spiked. "For thousands of years the natives have been reared in the belief that human sacrifices are indispensable for the propitiation of their gods; and it will take more than a few years to root out the belief that the absence of such offerings will necessarily be attended by drought, famine, and other terrible calamities."[1]

From what has been said it will be inferred that the pagans believe in a future state; hence they invoke the spirits of their deceased relatives to protect them. This notion accounts for the great reverence they pay to dead bodies,[2] which are dressed in the best attire procurable, and adorned with gold or aggrey beads, the belief being that the dead use in the other world those things which are put on and interred with them.[3] I have witnessed the interment of a pagan when a libation of trade gin was poured upon the ground, and an earnest prayer was offered to the spirit of the deceased not to come and torment the sorrowing friends. On the death of a rich man a number of slaves were killed, in the belief that they would be his attendants in the world of spirits.

[1] Mr. Hesketh J. Bell, address to Liverpool Chamber of Commerce May 1, 1893.
[2] I have seen the fingers of a corpse almost covered with handsome gold rings.
[3] Interments were usual in dwelling-houses, presumably for the greater safety of the jewellery, which was a great temptation to midnight gravediggers. The custom has very wisely been prohibited by the Government.

It will be of interest to know that the natives are decidedly of opinion that his highness of the lower regions has a white complexion. In *A Description of Guinney* are the following stanzas :—

> "The land of Negroes is not far from thence,
> Nearer extended to th' Atlantick main,
> Wherein the Black Prince keeps his Residence
> Attended with his Jeaty-coloured Train,
> Who in their native beauty most delight,
> And in contempt do paint the Devil white."

The Fetish priest is naturally an important personage among his people. Endowed with a marvellously retentive memory (as indeed is the case with all natives) he makes himself acquainted with the history and movements of his fellows, and is in a position to surprise them with his extraordinary knowledge of their affairs; this knowledge he is always careful to attribute to his communications with the Fetish deity to whose service he is attached. Scarcely a year passes without conversions to Christianity among the Fetish priests, on which occasions a clean breast is made of their deception.

It may after all well be doubted whether Fetishism has a very real hold on the natives of the Colony. It is true that even on the seaboard, where Christianity is represented in almost every town and village, we observe offerings devoted to the Fetish. These offerings, by the way, are usually of such a paltry character that no one would dream of taking the trouble to collect them as curiosities; and the devotees themselves smile at their own observance of the customs of their fathers. I do not for one moment suggest that distrust of Fetishism is necessarily followed by the adoption of the Christian faith. It is greatly to be regretted that the disproportion between Fetish renegades and Christian converts is very great, and the number appears to be increasing. Half a century ago it was feared that atheism would mark the transition stage. Experience, however, teaches that indifference is the principal characteristic. We have the growing conviction that with Christian agencies at work proportionate with those of England, the results would be a thousand per cent. greater.

And now a word respecting the introduction of past and present Christian agencies in the Colony. According to Dr. Blyden, the prince of African scholars, "the King of Portugal sent, in 1481, ten ships with five hundred soldiers, one hundred labourers, and a proper complement of priests as missionaries to Elmina," from which spot Christian knowledge and civilisation spread to other parts of the coast. The Portuguese missions, however, were entirely abandoned in time; for, from the year 1723 nothing was heard of them; they were given up, and "disappeared from West Africa."

In 1751, a clergyman, the Reverend Thomas Thompson, with a heart moved with pity at the wretched condition of the natives, sacrificed the prospects of a comfortable living in England in order that he might proclaim among the heathen the unsearchable riches of Christ. As far as we are able to gather from the records of those times, Mr. Thompson's health failed at the end of four years, and he returned to England with three negro youths, intending to have them educated and trained as missionaries to their fellows. Two of them died, after a short residence in England; the third, Philip Quacoe, spent nine years in London and Oxford, and was duly ordained and returned to Cape Coast in 1765. His work does not appear to have been successful, for after fifty years of service there were no visible results; indeed it is said that Quacoe himself died trusting as much in his Fetish as in Christ. After a few years' further trial, the Society for the Propagation of the Gospel, under whose direction Quacoe was appointed, decided to abandon the mission.

The Anglican Church is now represented only by the colonial chaplain at Accra and an assistant colonial chaplain at Cape Coast. In 1841 the Society for the Propagation of the Gospel suggested the advisability of sending an Anglican missionary to Ashanti: but, on the advice of Sir Thomas Dyke Acland and the Church Missionary Society, it was decided to leave to our own Society the field we were already holding, as we, on our part, left the Niger sphere of operations to the Church Missionary Society. Sir Thomas was afraid that "the appearance of two kinds of missionaries would prove a stumbling-block to the Ashantis."

The Basle, Lutheran, Mission work was begun in 1828, in Accra, and is, generally speaking, limited to the eastern part of the Colony, but has recently opened in the Ashanti country. The North German Mission was begun in 1847, and includes the eastern part of our own Colony and the western part of the neighbouring German Colony of Togoland.

Our own Mission was begun in 1834, at the suggestion of Captain Potter, of Bristol, who very generously gave a passage on one of his trading voyages, to our first missionary, the Reverend Joseph Dunwell. The mortality among the early missionaries was truly appalling. To-day we have churches in every town on the coast, from the western boundary to Adda, at the mouth of the Volta, and also in the interior districts of Wassaw, Assin, Adansi, Ashanti, Akim and Pekyi.

The Lyons Roman Catholic Mission was established at Elmina in 1881, and has important centres at Cape Coast, Anamabu, Salt Pond and Accra.

CHAPTER III

CONTAINS A REVELATION TO THE AUTHOR, THE STUDY OF WHICH PROVES THAT THE MISSIONARY'S PRECONCEIVED IDEAS RESPECTING HIS VOCATION DID NOT HARMONISE WITH HIS ACTUAL EXPERIENCE—SUGGESTIONS ARE ALSO RESPECTFULLY OFFERED TO THE ASPIRING WEST AFRICAN RESIDENT IN REFERENCE TO THE PRESERVATION OF HEALTH, AND THE READER IS INTRODUCED TO AN INVALUABLE COLLEAGUE

IT is difficult at this period to remember what was the exact idea of missionary methods one expected to adopt in Africa. I certainly remember that the picture presented to my mind was that of a missionary clad in white apparel, with wide-brimmed hat and umbrella, in close proximity to a cocoa-nut tree, and a concourse of dusky hearers about him. Broadly speaking, life was to be to me as different from what I had imagined as it was possible to be. My good superintendent gave me excellent advice, which I will pass on to those who have hopes of residing in Western Africa as missionaries : " Form no plans ; imitate nobody, but just do the work that comes most natural to you. The Committee has no cast-iron policy so long as the Gospel is preached : the freest scope is given to all missionaries." Let me also commend to the notice of my readers the experience of that veteran West African missionary when he says that, "apparently, there are three necessary stages through which the worker passes: the first is one of great enthusiasm and hope; the second is one of disappointment bordering on to disgust, at the unsatisfactory results of one's work; the third is reached only after the exercise of patience and kindly consideration for the surroundings of those among whom we work—it is a stage of utmost confidence in the ultimate success of the Gospel."

But, as we have now arrived at Cape Coast, we must disembark. Descending by means of a perpendicular rope ladder by the side of the ship, which is anchored half-a-mile from the landing-place, the new arrival is enjoined to watch a favourable opportunity for alighting in the surf-boat, so as to avoid getting his foot crushed. Our Fanti boatmen, whose clothing consists of a couple of yards of Manchester print tied round their waists, are well accustomed to their work, and will take us safely through the dangerous surf. If they are in a particularly happy mood, or have expectations concerning your "dash" (the Coast equivalent for the elegant word "tip"), they will sing your praises with the greatest enthusiasm, and will convey you most tenderly from the boat to the beach.

The Castle attracts our attention. It was built by the Portuguese in 1624, and was enlarged by the English in 1662, having in the meantime passed

CAPE COAST CASTLE. COMPANIES OF WEST INDIAN SOLDIERS.

[*To face page* 23.

"Our Fanti boatmen... ..will convey you most tenderly from the boat to the beach."

through the hands of the Dutch. This historic building is perfectly useless for purposes of defence ; the formidable looking cannon on the battlements have long since been condemned ; but there is ample accommodation for colonial officers, and men of the Houssa force.

On our way to the Mission House we observe the "severely Africo-Gothic structure," Wesley Chapel, a building of which we, in common with our native friends, are justly proud. Our house is described as a "palatial residence." The central block was purchased from a merchant half a century ago for an incredibly small sum of money ; and was enlarged at a period when the annual financial grant to the district was three hundred per cent. greater than it is now. Here the annual District Synod is held, when the European missionaries from the various parts of the district are in residence. Our dining-room has accommodation for thirty-five ministers and laymen in council. On the ground floor of the right wing we have an invaluable auxiliary to mission work in the form of a book depot. The idea originated with the Rev. W. M. Cannell in 1882. In 1887 the sales amounted to £422, and at the following Synod, a grant of £50 was made to various funds. If we may anticipate subsequent developments it will be gratifying to note that in 1893 the sales amounted to over £1,150. From the profits £100 was paid to district funds, and a balance of £90 was brought forward to 1894. The following year a printing-press and set of type, of the value of £120 were purchased, and have been successfully worked. We were enabled to print quantities of forms for the Army Pay Office during the Ashanti expedition of 1895-6. In addition to the substantial financial grants to the District Extension Fund and the Native Supernumerary Ministers' and Widows' Fund, the Book Room confers incalculable benefits on the district by its choice assortment of books, stationery and school materials. European visitors passing Cape Coast have been agreeably surprised to find their wants supplied in our bookseller's shop. The management of the depot was, in 1896, transferred from the senior European minister to the superintendent of the Cape Coast circuit, who is assisted by a local committee.

We were greatly disappointed on learning that Mr. Cannell was under medical orders to leave by the earliest possible steamer. Mr. Cannell has taken a most important part in the history of the Gold Coast Mission. As a graduate of London University, and with special philological gifts, he was in every way qualified for the transliteration work to which he was drawn, and to which he devoted himself for four or five years. In those days the Sunday Schools were languishing for want of vernacular books, and in the day schools the younger scholars were learning to read English without having the remotest idea of the meaning of the words. This suggested the production of "Exercises" in Fanti-English. The value of these little works is attested by the fact that they have been sold in enormous numbers, and a reprint is on order at the time of writing.

Mr. Cannell next proceeded to prepare a dictionary. The purpose he kept in view was to give one spelling to each word, so that future translators might be guided in their work. It is needless to say that there were difficulties in furnishing equivalents to all English words necessary in the translation of the Scriptures. But it may be mentioned, in passing, that the difficulties were not nearly as great as in other languages that might be named. Although it has been found necessary, after the interval of twelve years, to revise, and, naturally, to enlarge the vocabulary, the Fantis are very grateful to Mr. Cannell for his invaluable work. When this was completed, an abridged translation of the *Pilgrim's Progress* was taken in hand, and was put through the press by the very generous assistance of the Religious Tract Society. This was done in order to furnish specimens of Fanti writing, and to provide food for the Sunday Schools. Attention was next given to the Bible. A translation committee was formed, whose duty it was to revise the translations of the various books by ministers and laymen of the district. The publication of Genesis and the four Gospels by the British and Foreign Bible Society, whose generous aid is beyond all words, was also accomplished. In his work Mr. Cannell was aided by the suggestions and hearty co-operation of the Reverends Andrew W. Parker and Jacob B. Anaman, native ministers, whose experience was simply indispensable. It may here be mentioned that in recent years the work of revising the translations of the whole Bible has been entrusted to Mr. Parker. The whole of the New Testament has been published, and the Old Testament is rapidly approaching completion.

One feels bound to explain that the reason that so little attention had previously been paid to this all-important branch of mission work arose from the mistaken idea of earlier missionaries that the English language would supersede the vernacular. It is quite true that our language is making enormous headway, that it is, indeed, the "Court" language of the whole Coast, and the anxiety of the young people to acquire a knowledge of it can be abundantly attested;[1] but millions in the interior of the Colony will pass away without ever having uttered a word of it.

We cannot speak too highly of the forethought of the devoted, self-sacrificing German missionaries in being far ahead of us in vernacular publications. But, unfortunately, their principal work has been carried on in a neighbourhood where a composite

---

[1] It is possible that the missionaries felt that by encouraging the study of the English language they would be introducing the converts to our literature.

INTERIOR OF WESLEY CHURCH, CAPE COAST.

language is spoken, so that their Twi translations are about as serviceable for general circulation among the Akan speaking tribes as would a composite translation of three distinct dialects of this country be for general circulation in England.

My first duty was to assist the general superintendent in auditing the accounts and preparing the schedules of the various stations for the Synod which was about to be held. Writing at a time when we have superintendents sending us accounts which are models of neatness, we marvel at the progress that has been made in this branch of missionary work. The first fortnight was a season of bewildering, hopeless confusion. Mr. Halligey was the greater sufferer; having due regard to my inexperience of the climate, he insisted on my retiring to rest before midnight; but he himself sat up till the small hours of the morning, striving to get order out of chaos. The second duty was to act as financial secretary: this *office*, by the way, is supposed not to exist in our foreign missions; but the work does, with a vengeance. Unless the unfortunate individual who does the work is a born accountant, or a paragon in his methods of bookkeeping, he stands a reasonable chance of being a loser. The Home Committee naturally recognises no losses, and the Stations are, very properly, careful to have credit for all amounts paid in, and justly claim the last farthing of their grants; and so the results of omissions must necessarily be borne by the chancellor of the exchequer. This part of my missionary work has temporarily made me "poor indeed." As the fault, or misfortune, is entirely one's own, one naturally submits; but I take the opportunity to suggest to all intending missionaries the probability of having to be responsible for the payment of sums of money, varying from threepence to a hundred pounds.

The third duty consisted in managing a very feeble high school, which was on the verge of extinction, and also an elementary school, which certainly was much more promising; but as I had not had a day's experience of teaching or of school management, I undertook the duties with fear and trembling. The fourth charge was the management of the aforesaid book depot, to account for the daily sales, superintend the orders, and make the necessary remittances to the London Book Room. The fifth, the charge of our soldiers of the West India regiment at the Castle and the Hospital. Last, but not least, the services at Wesley where the congregation could appreciate a good sermon, though I feel bound to confess that the friends must have been sorely disappointed.

By way of recreation there was the management of the household. One naturally looked wondrous wise in giving directions to the cook; and it gave a little variety to life to keep an eye on the steward, who was not over particular in his use of the broom and duster, while his attempts at washing the linoleum gave the appearance of working with a grainer's comb and muddy water; and, in spite of our remonstrances, we found, every few days, that our clothing, boots, and books had become mildewy through neglect. In addition there were endless repairs and painting needed about the house and premises. It will easily be understood that at the end of each day it was found that "something had been attempted, something done, to earn a night's repose." In the meantime the ideal missionary with a flannel suit, cotton umbrella, etc. vanished completely from my vision.

I have hesitated in introducing the subject of personal health in this chapter. On the one hand I am tempted to hasten on to furnish an account of missionary work; on the other hand I feel that the subject of personal existence at the Gold Coast is, if possible, of greater importance. Let me therefore give an account of the mode of life, and also respectfully offer a suggestion as to the preservation of health. Again I must anticipate; and again I must remind the general reader that I am assuming that some who read these lines will one day visit the Gold Coast.

As Cape Coast is only four degrees north of the Equator there is very little difference between the length of day or night at any part of the year. Hence it was our practice to rise at six o'clock. Our earliest exercises were at the bath: it must be mentioned, however, that the majority of our fellow countrymen prefer their "tub" later in the day—after business hours. It is usual to take a cup of cocoa, some very light food, and fruit, at seven o'clock; and a substantial meal at eleven. Medical men who have not seen our poultry and farm-yards abroad warn us against eating carneous food in the tropics. But those who have partaken of our joints have no fears respecting harmful results; their only concern is whether the tough, leathery substance can possibly contain any nourishment at all. Dinner is at half-past seven. Fruit is not, as a rule, taken late in the day. Although the variety of fruit is not as great as in England, there is usually a fair supply of pineapples, bananas, oranges, mangoes, limes, alvacador pears, guavas and papaws.

And now a word or two as to the preservation of health. Here I may, at least, express the hope that the Government, the English merchants and our missionary society will, ere long, follow the excellent example of the Basle and the French Roman Catholic Societies, and allow no European worker to occupy a solitary station. In numberless ways companionship is unspeakably beneficial, but especially in time of sickness. The late Professor Drummond has said "that there is a stage in African fever—and every one must have fever—when the watchful hand of a friend may make all the difference between life and death."

My remarks are simply those of a layman, but

of one who has enjoyed on the whole very fair health, and who has had the privilege of ministering to the fever-stricken patients on scores of occasions, both with and without medical aid. The first suggestion is, avoid *needless* exposure to sun and rain. The heat, perhaps, is not as great at the Gold Coast as in some other tropical countries, but the effect upon a system which is more or less saturated with malaria may be far more deadly. Our native friends tell us that they incur quite as much risk in coming to England as we do in visiting their country. I can well understand that our cold is quite as trying to their constitutions as is their heat to us; but they altogether leave out of account their malaria, which is as "pestilence walking in darkness, and destruction wasting at noonday."

After exposure which has resulted in wet clothing, change the latter with the least possible delay, taking care to rub yourself with a rough towel. On these occasions take five or ten grains of quinine—the exact quantity will depend upon your general use of it. There are those who are able to boast that they can dispense with the drug for five or six months at a time. Others take small quantities frequently—in the wet season, daily. A medical friend, of considerable experience and success, tells me that fifty grains, taken during three consecutive days once a month, gives a sudden and salutary check to all malarial tendencies.

It is of the utmost importance to avoid remaining

in the vicinity of newly turned-up soil. It is important too not to over-estimate one's strength, or under-estimate the treachery of the climate. Many an inexperienced man has boasted that he "never felt better in his life," and has hinted that he was quite prepared to stay at his post for four or five years; but has very speedily found, to his sorrow, that he was reckoning without his host,—he has either been invalided home or his remains have been taken to the cemetery.

If one has been accustomed to live without stimulants, it is advisable not to take them unless specially prescribed by the medical attendant. Some men, indeed, have paid the penalty of over-indulgence by an early death; but the number of these is not proportionately great. On the other hand, even the most carefully regulated lives succumb to the terrible fever. The most scrupulous total abstainers are of opinion that alcohol, in one form or another, though perhaps not necessary in this land, cannot always be dispensed with yonder. But the man who has not grace to control his appetite should certainly avoid the Gold Coast; for in that thirsty land the temptations naturally are very great: and without the restraining influences of wife, mother, or sister, a man's life may become such as to cause those of his old home to blush.

In addition to the precautionary suggestions may I advise generous living, plenty of work—not to the extent of exhaustion—and regular exercise as the means to be employed for the preservation of health? But your magnificent constitution, your indomitable pluck, the exercise of your most prudent judgment will not ensure absolute immunity from the malaria. Suppose I give an account of my own "seasoning"! The experience then gained may be of service to others. The attack, which was the most persistent and painful that I had, came upon me during my fifth month of residence. It was on a Sunday morning, the violent pains in my head and back made me heartily wish that I had not to preach. But it was not until some hours later, when my worthy colleague suggested the advisability of taking my temperature, that it was discovered that the clinical thermometer registered 102°. How much higher the temperature might have risen, or how much more difficult it would have been to have grappled with the attack, but for Mr. Hall's timely suggestion and help, it is, of course, impossible to say. There is no doubt that it would have been a much more serious matter. Of course the doctor was summoned. "Doctor not at home!" It was quite a new experience for us. But we proved that "a little knowledge" is *not necessarily* "a dangerous thing!" The first business was to secure the action of the liver, which had become torpid, and at the same time to open the pores of the skin—nature's safety-valves. But they were very obstinate—as they always are in such cases; and although the temperature of the bedroom was at 75°—it was in the wet season and consequently cool—I was miserably cold. In addition to the flannel sleeping-suit, there were three blankets and a rug placed over me, and two hot-water bottles at my feet, and then to supplement the tumblers of exceedingly hot lime-juice, my friend insisted on my taking the most vile drug that man ever invented—Warburg's Fever Tincture. All this was done to arrest the temperature, which rose to 104° before the doctor arrived. Mr. Hall had the satisfaction of knowing that his methods were perfectly in accordance with medical knowledge ; and for this he thanks the Didsbury College authorities, who arranged the medical course for the missionary students. Those days were days of heroic doses of quinine. I took three hundred grains in five days before the temperature was reduced to its normal condition.

Native friends were very kind; some of them insisted on taking nights on duty. I shall ever be grateful for the kindness shown on that occasion. Our worthy factotum was as gentle as a woman in his movements. During the stages of convalescence friends sent presents of fruits, and on the first Sunday after recovery no fewer than sixteen visitors called—including six soldiers, who came to wish me " very much good evening!"

One remarkable feature about a malarial fever is the suddenness of a change for the better, or worse. One day one hears that so-and-so has an attack of fever; the next day he is dead, the next morning buried. Or the man who was down with a dose yesterday is attending to his papers in his bedroom to-day, and expects to be in his office to-morrow. Or again, an invalid is put on board a vessel in an apparently dying state; it is feared that he will not live to see Sierra Leone or Grand Canary: but, to the surprise of every one but the invalid—and he has not bothered his head about such a trifling matter—he does linger and live, and by the time he gets to Liverpool he is quite himself again; and then comes the unkindest cut of all: "What in the world have you come home for?"

I have already mentioned, though in an unpardonably unceremonious manner, the name of a colleague to whom I owe a debt of gratitude for kindness shown in time of sickness. My friend, the Reverend S. C. Hall and I have ever agreed that never were two more dissimilar colleagues brought together. We differed in appearance; the illiterate natives, who did not take the pains to pronounce our by-no-means-unpronounceable names, referred to Mr. Hall as the military, and to me as the medical, looking missionary. By the way, in those days I was known as the "little white man!" Seeing that I stand a shade over six feet in my stockings, I ought to add that the diminutive term had reference purely to my relative importance. Our—I was going to say *literary* tastes, but it would be more accurate to say our—libraries differed. It was always a very great pleasure to hear my friend discussing, with a kindred spirit, the works and worth of countless authors from the times of Chaucer. My own scant literary tastes were confined, almost exclusively, to theology and sermons. My wife declares that, in later times, my first request, on recovering from an attack of fever, was for a volume of Pope's *Theology*. My friend had an easy, graceful flow of speech; mine was laboured and slow. Our methods of work differed; but then I soon found that I was to learn much from one whom I regard as a model organiser.

The duties assigned to Mr. Hall were the temporary charge of the Cape Coast Church, which had a thousand members, while the native superintendent took a much-needed rest for six months. This work involved, among other duties, the weekly attendance at the Leaders' Meeting, where the names on the Church roll were carefully examined, and a wholesome sifting ensued. In addition, there was the oversight of the Sunday Schools, with preparation classes for teachers, the charge of the Bible Translation Committee, and the formation of a Theological Class for our local preachers. The Sunday School sorely needed attention. I have clear recollections of the deplorable condition of things which my friend discovered. There seemed to have been a tacit understanding, on the part of scholars and teachers alike, that it was quite the correct thing to take a month's holiday at the beginning of the year, as will be gathered from Mr.

Hall's diary. "January 29, '88. Visited school for first time. The greatest confusion prevails; only one teacher and twenty children present at the opening service; total numbers present later, seventy-seven; total names on registers, one hundred and thirty-two." Mr. Hall speedily set to work and secured additional teachers, and framed rules for the guidance of the school. In response to his exertions, the *regular attendance* at the end of May numbered four hundred, and the names of *one hundred* young people were enrolled as candidates for "junior" Church membership. What a contrast to the feeble spectacle at the beginning of the year! From that time forward the school advanced by leaps and bounds, and proved a stimulus to all our schools in the district. Mr. Hall's personal friends furnished the necessary means for the formation of a lending library in connection with the school. But I am sorry to have to say that the enthusiasm of the readers was not maintained for a great length of time.

Early in April it was found necessary to dispense with the services of the superintendent of the Anamabu Churches. Mr. Hall was appointed to the charge. And so, in addition to taking over his responsible duties, I was deprived of his companionship. But as his new centre was only ten miles from Cape Coast, we frequently saw one another. His solitude, however, was intensified by the fact that there were no Europeans residing at Anamabu. And the discomforts in his new home! On referring to the diary, which has been placed at my disposal, I find—

"The experience of April 11th will live with me as long as memory itself. The first serious journey, with all the novelty of the travelling chair borne on men's heads; the bush and the forest; the village, with the stench from the fish ovens; the sleeping crocodile on the banks of the lagoon; the dilapidation of the town; the old school with its tree inside high above where the roof should have been; the house with its rotten verandahs; women smoking short clay pipes, their oily skin flooded with perspiration.

"The house has been deserted for some time; the white ants have attacked the floor, and dry rot has set in. When I put my foot upon the floor it went below, as also did three of the legs of the chair in which I attempted to sit. The roof served little purpose but for the study of astronomy. The house swarmed with mosquitos; and the 'kotokrodu,' in legions, had taken up their abode in the missionary's bed chamber. There were myriads of black ants conveying mud from my wells to make themselves a home in my rooms. On sweeping the floor, by means of a plank placed cross-wise, I removed bucketfuls of refuse, and in so doing disturbed swarms of beetles, many of them as big as miniature clock-weights. There were rats galore, and one snake. There was a vampire, which I succeeded in securing; it measures twelve inches by two! I had been sent to a mission house, but I found something approaching a menagerie.

"Night came on, but it was made hideous by the unearthly yells of a pair of jackals. Dropping upon an old bed which had seen no linen for a long time, I gathered the mosquito curtain around me, and essayed to sleep. But I had made my calculations without reckoning with the buzz of the mosquitos, and the visits of the rats. I had thought that the bed was for my use; but a mother of the rodent tribe and her family were there to dispute the point with me. As, however, might and right prevailed, my visitors took their revenge on my underclothing, and left by the morning little but buttons and, as the Irishman says, 'a bundle of holes stitched together."

"But with the opening day came officials and members of the Church, with their presents of yams, eggs, oranges, bananas, fowls, fish, etc. and in so doing they gave to their missionary a right royal African welcome; and by their loyalty to the great Head of the Church through many trying circumstances, they greatly endeared themselves to me."

There were special matters affecting the Church which rendered Mr. Hall's visits to Cape Coast particularly welcome to me. We shall treat of one such in our next chapter. On the occasion of these visits we surprised our native friends by the novelty of our recreation, which at times took the form of tree-felling and general horticultural pursuits. Our worthy factotum protested that "the natives would not like to see" us do that kind of work. I do not think that manual labour was considered by them to be an undignified employment for us; but I thought then, as I do now, that the educated natives might with advantage teach the young people by example that manual labour is not necessarily degrading. Occasionally we took exercise in a walk along the Ashanti, or Elmina road, or in a paddle along the lagoon. Once we set out to explore the ruins of Fort Nassau, built by the Dutch in 1624, at Mouree, six miles to the east of Cape Coast. The loose sand by the sea-shore proved rather more fatiguing than we had imagined, and accordingly we shortened our journey. We were grimly compensated for our eight-mile walk by finding two adult skeletons, said to be those of Fetish priests, who were usually buried by the shore.

At times our inclination led us through the town, which is an odd intermixture of native huts and houses more or less of European style. In the part where the poorer classes live the houses are terribly huddled together; and as the roofs are flat, and the mud walls have no lime plaster, their general appearance suggests a recent bombardment. The two principal streets of Cape Coast are wide, with a range of wild fig or umbrella trees planted on each side. These afford shade, and at the same time greatly improve the appearance of the thoroughfares.

On the 1st of June the *Akassa* came into port. We were greatly surprised to receive a note from Bryan Roe, who was on his way to Grand Canary. We went aboard, and found that our friend had been unconscious the previous ten days. It is difficult to realise that five months' residence on the Coast could have made such a wreck of a man. He must have had an "awful turn," as we sometimes say on the Coast; for Mr. Halligey had written a letter for the servant to give me, with instructions as follows:—" I am sending poor Roe by the *Akassa*. If he is better, and is able to go on, cable 'Gone.' If he is able to stay with you, say 'Better.' If you are obliged to go to Sierra Leone with him, say 'Left.' If he is *dead*, which God forbid, say 'Dead.' Our friend was able to go on without me. One sentence he uttered made an indelible impression on our minds. It was, "Nature sometimes allows a good deal of slack rope in Africa, but it is hauled in sooner or later!"

CHAPTER IV

DEALS WITH THE DIFFICULTIES IN INTRODUCING CHRISTIAN IDEAS RESPECTING MARRIAGE—REFLECTIONS CONCERNING THE CHARACTER OF THE NATIVE, AND REFERENCES TO OUR SCHOOL AT CAPE COAST

IN the early part of our residence at Cape Coast we were brought face to face with one of the gravest difficulties with which the missionary has to deal. I refer to our relation as a Church to the native marriage laws. Discussion at our annual Synods on this question has occupied much time and thought. But, as we have now arrived at a decision which is likely to help us out of the difficulty, it may be of interest to make more than a passing reference to the subject.

It will easily be understood that, in a land where polygamy [1] has been observed from time immemorial, Christian marriage laws sometimes prove most irk-

---

[1] I ought to remark that I by no means share the views of those who regard polygamy as an insuperable barrier to the progress of Christianity. It is quite possible that our accessions to the Church would be greatly increased if we admitted polygamists. But, on the other hand, it must be stated that we are constantly receiving kings and chiefs who have to do violence to the wishes of their people in complying with the laws of the Church.

some to candidates for Church membership. At the same time it will also be understood that pagan ideas respecting the sanctity of marriage are hardly in harmony with scriptural teaching on the subject.

Recommendations and legislation of the Synod have been progressive. In 1875 it was decided to "discountenance the payment of 'dowries' after pagan customs; extravagant expenditure in marriage feasting and bridal attire; or any practice or custom inconsistent with the circumstances of the parties and out of harmony with a true Christian spirit and deportment." It may, perhaps, sound strange that there should be an objection to the "dowry"; but the word is misleading to English readers. The custom is, I believe, supposed to have been handed down from patriarchal times—from the times when it was necessary to work a number of years to win a bride, or to take costly presents to the lady and her friends. And so it has come to pass that the bridegroom has to pay an ounce or two of gold to the family of the bride—the price varies according to the social position of the respective parties—in addition to presents of wearing apparel. The result really is that the bride is *purchased*;[1] the word does

---

[1] On one occasion we were seated in the house of a catechist when a poor girl came to our host in tears, imploring him to intercede with her friends on her behalf. It seems that she was hoping to be wed to a Christian young man who was prepared to pay the ordinary dowry, but another had come with a more tempting offer, and her friends had intimated that she must go to the higher bidder.

not sound pleasant, but we can use no other. Indeed, one objection to the Christian rite of marriage is that the property of the bridegroom, who may be the head of an old and influential family, thus passes from the family to one who came into the domestic circle "with hardly a rag or stitch." How perfectly natural that native laws in harmony with this custom should sanction the dismissal of the wife, on the ground, say, that she was diseased and disfigured or incapable of performing her duties![1] Again, how necessary it was to discountenance extravagance in bridal attire may be judged by the fact that on occasions young men in receipt of a stipend of £50 a year have actually *fooled*—there really is no other word—away as much as £60 in purchasing a bridal trousseau in England,[2] to say nothing of the settlement with the family. No explanation, perhaps, is necessary respecting the Synod's disapproval "of any practice out of harmony with a true Christian spirit and deportment."

In 1885 the Synod decided that "no member of the Church should be allowed to marry a heathen man or woman; and no woman, being a member of

---

[1] A professing Christian man once endeavoured to point out to me the advantage of taking a wife according to the laws of the country. It was suggested that an opportunity was thus afforded for ascertaining if the parties suited one another. Fancy taking a wife, like a sewing machine, on a month's free trial!

[2] It will be a revelation to our readers to know that our native friends imagine that this is an English custom!

A Neat Head-dress.

Preparing a Meal.

[To face page 50.

the Church, should be allowed to marry a man who already had a wife; both these being scriptural principles." Further, "no man having more than one wife should be admitted as a member of our Church, and that it should be left with the superintendent minister to decide whether, on an investigation of the case, the wives of polygamists should be received into Church fellowship." It will be understood that, as the bride was not always consulted in making the matrimonial arrangement, special consideration was shown to such on their application for Church membership. I remember an instance where the marriage of a girl with a polygamous king was arranged by her friends. On embracing Christianity the wife, now grown to womanhood, voluntarily resolved to leave the king, who demanded from her the sum of money which had been paid to her friends. She had not wherewith to pay; accordingly, the handful of really poor Christians living in the village raised the money from among themselves and paid the debt.

The Synod of 1890 made the following recommendations:—First, "that the perfect mutual agreements of the parties proposing to marry should be imperatively insisted on;" second, "that the consent of the parents of both parties is highly desirable, and should, if possible, be obtained;" third, "that there should be no extravagant expenditure. A breach of this regulation should render the offending parties amenable to discipline."

The Synod of 1893 decided, after much earnest thought, to insist on the Christian rite of marriage.

During the years that the whole question has been under discussion we have, at the request of our people, been in correspondence with the Government, and have succeeded in lessening the difficulties that have stood in the way of observing the Christian rite. Hence the number of registrars has been increased—it is no longer necessary for the ardent lover to trudge a distance of two hundred miles to get his certificate; a great number of our chapels have been licensed for the solemnization of marriage; the respective families have not now to spend a week in journeying to and from the scene of the sacred rite; the registration fees have been reduced. Altogether the Governors, past and present, have earned our gratitude for the patience with which they have considered our applications.

Although our Church has insisted on the observance of the Christian rite of marriage as a condition of membership, consideration is shown to those who are not at present prepared to take so great a step. "In order to ease the situation members married according to the native law are permitted to be received *on trial* for membership, on the distinct understanding that they cannot pass beyond the trial stage until they conform to the Christian rite."

An old gentleman came to our house some six or seven years ago to ask if we would arrange for the solemnisation of the marriage service of his son, who was a clerk at a Government office some twenty miles from Cape Coast. It was explained that the young man could leave his work only on one particular day. We very gladly promised to make the necessary arrangements. Just as he was leaving us the old gentleman volunteered the information that he had "looked out" a girl for his son. The idea occurred to us that the expression could not be taken too literally, inasmuch as the applicant was *stone blind!* The wonder to us has ever been how he was able to judge of the qualities of the bride-elect.

Thursday is, I believe, considered the "lucky day" for the celebration of marriages. I know of only one departure from the rule; and, sadly enough, both the bride and bridegroom, who were held in the highest esteem by a large circle of European and native friends, died within a year of the wedding day.

Some of our happiest evenings in Africa have been spent at the wedding feasts given by the parents of the bride. Our hosts on these occasions have been gentlemen of wealth, else we might have wondered at the bountiful provision set before us.

Opinions respecting the character of the natives vary according to the experience or temperament of those who are brought into contact with them. On the one hand there are those who indiscriminately brand the negroes as the craftiest and the basest of beings on the face of the earth; it is always safe to allow very generous discounts on statements furnished by such travellers. On the other hand there are those who place the greatest confidence in the natives. "I never bother about my keys. I don't even know what money I have about me. Leave all such matters with the 'boy'"! Such are the remarks one sometimes hears from the Government officer or trader. I am bound to say that such a manifestation of confidence is neither wise nor kind. Strange as it may appear, the missionary can relate most varied, and, apparently, contradictory experiences. It would be quite possible, for example, by a narration of actual fact, to lead one's auditors to suppose that one's work was accompanied by unparalleled success—but only one who is lacking either in intelligence or in principle would give such a partial version of experience. On the other hand, one might with equal truth unfold such a tale of woe as would most certainly lead to the inquiry, "Does missionary work among a people so depraved warrant the enormous outlay of men and money?"—but such a revelation would be given only by the shortsighted, or the snob. The safest course lies between these extremes. We should be guilty of the gravest injustice, not merely to the supporters of missions, but to the natives themselves, if we entirely ignored the weaknesses and vices which are so manifest in the heathen world. But at the end of the recital of our gloomiest experiences we must, if we are honest, utter words full of hope and encouragement.

What is the raw material like? It surely was an altogether fanciful picture that described how—

> "The naked negro panting at the line,
> Boasts of his golden sands and palmy wine,
> Basks in the glare, or stems the tepid wave,
> And thanks the gods for all the good they gave."

Here violent exertion and gratitude are suggested; but we look in vain for them in the average native.

" Clean in their persons, but dirty in their habits," is the opinion generally expressed concerning the Gold Coast natives. They revel in their bath, but their homes or huts are often very filthy. The profusion of ill odours meeting one on entering their huts, and the questionable messes served as food and devoured with nasty fingers, are revolting to our ideas of cleanliness. I am afraid, too, that we must regard the race as indolent,[1] the exceptions are among those who have ambition to rise above their surroundings. I have made use of a word which I feel almost tempted to recall; for, after all, one does not wonder at the disinclination to manual labour. The softness of the climate is enervating; the few wants of man are met in the fertile soil, it would therefore be gratuitous to work. Their preference

[1] On one occasion I carried a rather heavy gun-carriage wheel from the front to the back of the house, in doing so I had to pass up two flights of steps, altogether a distance of forty yards; I then requested a young man to carry it to the tool house, a distance of twelve yards. He promptly called three youths to help him.

for ease has become as much a part of themselves as their physical features, and they are in consequence as little blameworthy as is a tortoise for its slowness. I think it is Dr. Parker who says that when God cursed the ground for man's sake, and thus made him seek his food by the sweat of his brow, He really sent a blessing in disguise. I heartily endorsed that sentiment before I went to Africa, but now I am inclined to think that the happiness of the average negro could not be increased by protracted toil. Gold may be obtained, and yet they seldom exert themselves in search of it. Forests, rich in possibilities, hem them in on all sides; here timber, oil, fibre, and rubber grow uncultivated. But this soil, which might vie with the whole world in its yield of dried fruits, is allowed to breed only miasma and death.

The power to initiate or originate is not largely developed, and yet they possess much native cunning. Their skill in adulteration is well known; it is possible that their forefathers acquired the art from Europeans, but certainly the pupil has learnt to excel the master. In all business transactions with Europeans the negro is generally competent to take care of himself. The power to imitate is most marvellous. A goldsmith will make an exact copy of an elaborately designed piece of European jewellery. Work in leather, wood, stone, iron, copper and silver is astonishing to those who expect to find in the native only uncouth savagery. But

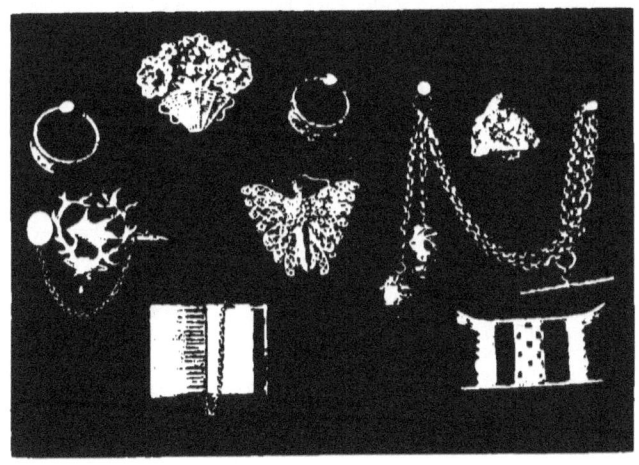

NATIVE GOLDSMITH'S WORK.

GOLD BROOCHES AND RINGS.   NUGGET.
LADY'S ALBERT WITH AGGREY BEADS.
SILVER STOOL KNIFE REST.

GA CHIEF'S GOLD BREAST ORNAMENTS.   [*To face page* 36.
(ORIGINALS SEVEN INCHES IN DIAMETER. INTRINSIC VALUE, £50.)

this gift is a great snare; its cultivation might make good workmen, but as a matter of fact it is allowed to develop into forgery or trickery which ends in the gaol. To many the white man is the example, but too often only the weaknesses are imitated.

It has been observed that their love for their offspring and their profound respect and reverence for the aged are marked traits in their character. This is certainly the case, but we look in vain for "that generous integrity of nature and honesty of disposition which always augurs true greatness, and is usually accompanied with undaunted courage and resolution"—manliness. Cowardice is one of their most serious defects. In warfare they have become a byword among those who have commanded them; they are ever ready to obtain an advantage over the weak. Their savagery becomes manifest in their outrages on their dead foes. Untruthfulness is transmitted at birth; "they go astray as soon as they are born, speaking lies." Their supreme concern is in grovelling sycophancy. But does not this carry back the mind to the dark passages in their history, by no means remote, when these poor people were in the hands of fell tyrants, whose amusement was murder, whose toys were knives or clubs? Does not all this remind us of the bloodstained page of their history when their forefathers abjectly crawled at the feet of some black Nero, on whose will or whim they were dependent for very life, and, in mortal fear, sought to utter—true or false, it mattered not which—words that would please him? Does it not recall the ravages of a horrible system of slavery, which in all its ferocity was carried on by civilised (?) white men as well as black for hundreds of years? Is it to be wondered that untruthfulness has become a national characteristic? Assuredly no! Shame on us, ten thousand times, if we regard these poor souls with anything but the tenderest pity!

We who have been enlightened and have the influence of centuries of civilisation behind us, dare not be severe upon our less favoured fellows. The marvel is, not that the natives of the Gold Coast have sunk so low, but that there is still remaining to them that which can lay hold of the pure religion of the Lord Jesus Christ.

Among our Gold Coast people there are distinctions greater than those which wealth can create. We have the unsophisticated bush man, and the coast man; the illiterate, and the scholar. The difference between the bushman and the coaster is almost as great as is the difference between our own Hodge and the town dandy. The bushman still retains "the primeval simplicity of his manners." He regards the white man as a living wonder, rivalled only by the horse, each being equally rare. He is most courtly in his welcome. His garb is simply a native cloth, like the Roman toga, thrown over the left shoulder, and hanging in folds down to his knees, or rolled round his waist.

During a heavy downpour of rain the cloth is carefully folded up and the owner indulges in a delicious shower bath. On such occasions, our friend, not being over conventional, cares little whether the fig leaf is worn round his waist or is growing on a tree miles away. He is convinced that Nature's garb is sufficient for Nature's gentlemen.

His town brother is poles removed from him. In many instances he has, through the enterprise of the merchant, and the encouragement of the Government, adopted European dress: this touches what to some is a sore spot. For my own part I am supremely indifferent in the matter of native dress, provided that due regard is paid to decency. It is true that there is an air of stateliness in the toga of the native; but it certainly was not designed with a view to ease and comfort when performing manual labour. It is equally true that educated natives, who avoid excesses in the matter of style, find European clothing as suitable as do Europeans themselves. But there is great tendency to carry the fashion to absurd lengths: the tall silk hat, high collar, patent leather shoes, must be as uncomfortable to the aristocrat, as the gorgeous Christy-minstrel attire of the humbler classes is grotesque. The coast gentleman usually requires the services of a boy to carry even the smallest parcel; a great number of retainers denotes importance.

Reference must be made to African royalty.

Our ideas of English royalty account for much misconception respecting African potentates. It will prove a great shock to those who have spoken with bated breath of West African princes to be told that some of us have engaged gentlemen bearing royal titles as bricklayers' labourers at wages of ninepence a day.[1] Much misconception concerning English royalty is also observed among our Gold Coast natives. It was once reported at Cape Coast in perfectly good faith that the Prince ——, when in England, was in the habit of calling every week to have a chat with Queen Victoria. But, unfortunately, the Governor of the Colony happened to tell the Queen that Prince —— was "no good!" So the next time that gentleman called at the Queen's house, her Majesty "shut the door in his face!"

Other distinctions are the "illiterate" and the "scholar." The former needs no explanation; but with regard to the latter it must be pointed out that our friend does not necessarily come within the category of divines and scientists of our own country. The "scholar" of the Gold Coast may have spent only sufficient time at school to enable him to write a misspelt letter, but still he is known by the title.

---

[1] Once upon a time his Majesty of ——, followed by a small retinue, called upon the missionary at Cape Coast. At the conclusion of the interview his Majesty begged for the sum of *sixpence*, to enable him to drink the missionary's health in gin; but as the latter had no faith in "trade spirits," he regaled his visitors with a bottle of dried currants.

[*To face page* 61.

GOLD COAST MATRONS AND CHILDREN.

"There is a pensiveness on the face when not excited, often passing to a languor and listlessness, which might suggest oppression had we not the conviction that they are resigned to their inferior position."

And yet another distinction must be named—the "lady" and the "woman." "My wife is a lady!" "Oh, indeed! What is the difference between a 'woman' and a 'lady'?" "The 'lady' wears a European dress, the 'woman' only wears cloth!" "Ladies," at least when in their advanced dress, do not perform all the menial duties that their less favoured sisters do. But generally speaking the gentler sex are industrious. Long before daybreak they may be heard grinding corn or beating fufu, or sweeping the hut or yard in order to be ready to go to the farm to prepare produce, or to the market to barter it. Very frequently they may be seen with fifty or sixty pounds weight of oil or rubber on their heads, and a babe on their backs, trudging uncomplainingly to town. I have seen a woman removing sacks of palm kernels weighing one hundred and forty pounds from warehouse to sea-shore. It is needless to say the poor soul required the assistance of another woman and man to enable her to lift the load to her head.

As a rule the women are cheerful and neighbourly; although often painfully shy in the company of white men, they are usually thoughtful and kind. There is a pensiveness on the face when not excited, often passing to a languor and listlessness, which might suggest oppression had we not the conviction that they are resigned to their inferior position. They are possessed of excitable dispositions, and are most demonstrative in affection and sorrow, and turbulent in dispute. Although hasty in speech and gesture, they are patient in suffering, and heroically struggle against disease.

Work in the day schools, which I had almost dreaded, became intensely fascinating. I must say that I possessed at least one essential qualification for this all-important work, and that was a very real love for the young people; and the love has been reciprocated. I have to confess that there were periods when it was impossible to avoid wounding the susceptibilities of some of the adult members of the community; but my young friends, with whom I was constantly brought into contact, never questioned my attachment to them.

What a motley company we had in the school!— the greatest variety in dress as well as in the stature of the scholars. Very often the dress consisted merely of a strip of Manchester cotton tied round the waist; and, by the way, this suit of clothes did duty on Sundays as well as during the week, by night as well as by day. In some instances jacket and trousers of blue winsey or bed-ticking made up a suit; others, again, had complete suits, all but shoes and socks. A sharp little fellow standing four feet high would be found by the side of a young man who bore signs of a moustache. "*You* an *infant!*" exclaimed an inspector to the latter. "Why, you ought to be *married!*" There was one very noticeable defect in our school, and that was the lamentable disproportion in the attendance of the girls. Very early it was noticed that there was sore need of an agitation for Women's Rights, of which more hereafter.

I made it a point of my duty to conduct a weekly examination in the senior classes. I found, as my predecessor had found, that there was a great tendency to learn to pronounce English words—in some instances with absurdly amusing results—without any thought of comprehending the meaning. There were also the daily lessons in Scripture. It was also found necessary to instil lessons on the value of time, and habits of punctuality: this is a heart-aching subject. With some of my young friends it was necessary to attend to the first principles of truthfulness and honesty. There are some dear good people in the world who charge the missionary with the responsibility of developing rogues and swindlers in West Africa. Why, in the name of Consistency, these dear good people do not charge the Sheffield cutlers with the responsibility of the human sacrifices at Kumasi because a Sheffield blade was found there altogether passes my comprehension. I am quite prepared to admit that the educated liar can carry out his schemes much more successfully than can the bushman.[1] Your cockney sharper is a much

---

[1] Even in England "a limited education has a tendency to increase crimes involving cupidity and corruption; for an imperfectly educated man, dishonestly inclined, is by his training afforded assistance in preparing and carrying out his fraudulent schemes, whether alone or in conspiracy with others, and in concealing his guilt and avoiding detection. My observation leads me to the belief that comparatively few

smarter man than is the rural thief. He has had his wits sharpened. But do not say that residence in London necessarily makes a man a thief. Your unsophisticated bushman does not make the attempts on your property that his town brother does, simply because he is afraid that something very dreadful will be the consequence, for in awe he regards you as a great white Fetish. But upon this subject I will now only add that every pupil in our school very quickly learnt that I was far more concerned that he should learn to speak the truth, "and keep his hands from picking and stealing," than that he should excel as a scholar.

In my educational work I had the invaluable assistance of a most devoted band of teachers, who were most painstaking with their work. One of them was in the habit of using grandiloquent language—this is a temptation to which so many of our educated young men at the Coast yield; but when I suggested that the sentence "—— has applied himself most assiduously to his scholastic duties," might be rendered in simpler English, the hint was taken, and I had no further occasion to draw attention to high-flown style.

persons are convicted of crimes of this description, but that many who have committed such crimes have managed to avoid detection by reason of the assistance their abused education has rendered to their cunning devices. Of course I cannot vouch for the correctness of my views; of necessity they are almost entirely speculative." Mr. Justice Hawkins' reply to the *New York World's* question, "Does not education increase crime?"

Among the earliest memorials laid before me was a request to support a petition by the teachers to the local committee for an increase of salaries, which were, indeed, wretchedly small. I had found that it was a general rule on the advent of Europeans for personal servants to request an increase on account of "the hardness of the times." But the request of the staff was certainly most reasonable. The pay-sheet of that time is one of the greatest curiosities in my collection. We honour the Mission Staff generally for the sacrifice they make in serving the cause they have at heart. But, really, that paysheet! I think I will not introduce it.

One of the little fellows attending our school found a particularly warm place in my heart. It was said that he had neither father nor mother, hence he was at once attached to our household. I had thought of one day bringing him to England; but subsequent experience confirmed the report of our faithful cook to the effect that "Dis boy, he get 'strong ears' dis time. He no speak fo' boys at school. He no wash plate!" On reflection I concluded that a trip to England might prove mistaken kindness.

Here I must record the greatest misfortune I have experienced in Africa, namely, my scant knowledge of the vernacular. At Cape Coast, where English is so much spoken, one does not realise the need of a knowledge of Fanti. Our catechists have a fair

F

knowledge of English;[1] our teachers are still more advanced; while our ministers, with one or two exceptions, have a perfect knowledge—at least, for all practical purposes. And so I imagined that there would be no need for me to apply myself to the study. And, besides, I knew so well that the average length of service of my predecessors had been so short that I feared that the time necessary for such study could ill be spared. But I would certainly recommend the study to others; not, perhaps, so much for the purpose of preaching—although if that state of proficiency could be attained it would be an unspeakable advantage—but in order to assist in comprehending the native mind and mode of reasoning. For, as the late Professor Drummond has said: "I often wished I could get inside an African for an afternoon, and just see how he looked at things; for I am sure our worlds are as different as the colour of our skins."

We had a Bible class on Sunday afternoons at the Mission House. During the study of the Epistle to the Ephesians we had an interesting discussion respecting social customs. Attention was drawn to the exhortation to husbands respecting the treatment of their wives, and it was unmistakably evident that some of the members felt that St. Paul

[1] We were once expressing to a German missionary our regret that our numberless duties prevented our giving attention to the study of the vernacular when our friend exclaimed, "And what need have you English to learn a foreign language, when you make every nation under the sun learn yours?"

was lavish in his gallantry. "But, sir," said one, "a Mandingo woman will not believe that her husband loves her unless he flogs her occasionally!" It was pointed out that it was not ours to discuss either Mandingo, or Fanti, or English customs; ours was to see that we observed Apostolic teaching, of regarding the wife as our own flesh. *À propos* of this it is said that a missionary (not a West African) once remonstrated with a member of his flock for having chastised his wife. The instant retort was, "Do not I read that 'whom the Lord loveth He chasteneth,' and do not I love my wife?"

A reference to my diary and letters reminds me that the initiation into the arts and mysteries of housekeeping at this period afforded considerable variety. New dusters and lamp-cloths were on one occasion needed, and were accordingly supplied. Shortly afterwards sounds of an altercation came from the kitchen, when it was discovered that the cook had allowed a pudding-cloth to get too near the fire, whereupon the steward's soiled lamp-cloth was demanded as a substitute, from which it will be inferred that the missionary must not be too inquisitive concerning the *cuisine*. There was a little difficulty in understanding the English as it was spoken at our house. My colleague's retainer was sent to me on one occasion for the loan of a "crecktill commonplay on Samuel." After a little thought I handed him the desired Critical Commentary.

CHAPTER V

GIVES AN ACCOUNT OF A JOURNEY INTO THE "BUSH," WITH GLIMPSES OF FOREST SCENERY, AND AN INTRODUCTION TO THE RURAL MEMBERS OF THE CHURCH

At the end of October my colleague arrived from a tour of his huge circuit. As he had been unwell for some days he suggested that I should try the novelty of "bush-travel," and at the same time supply his lack of service. I hesitated for a time, but have since been very thankful for that opportunity of seeing our interior work; it was most beneficial to me. As each day's journey was to be a very short one, not more than ten miles, four men were sufficient for the hammock,[1] and three carriers for boxes containing provisions, cooking utensils, and clothing. It may be mentioned that the wages of these men are at the rate of one shilling a day, with threepence each for "subsistence."

On the 2nd of November at 6 a.m. we set off. Our destination for that day was Anamabu. We

[1] It will be understood that as we have no railways, and no horses, bullocks nor mules, we have to submit ourselves to the humiliating process of being borne about the country in a hammock on the heads or shoulders of four men.

did not travel at express speed, for the ten miles occupied exactly four hours, but then there were one or two short halts by the way. The recumbent position in the hammock naturally induces sleep—the jolting jog-trot of the carriers notwithstanding. In your imagination you may be anywhere, travelling at a fearful speed. But you have a rude awakening—a sudden full-stop, and you hear the voice of the "head man," "Dis hill be no good, sah!" which, being interpreted, means, "Get out and walk!" At other times the ground is level, the road wide, a little way ahead is a densely-packed "bush market." There are a thousand of the gentler sex engaged in the exchange of plantain, peppers, palm wine, kassava, and other products too numerous to mention. The noise and chatter are beyond description! But it is a supreme moment in the history of the hammock men. With a sound that may be described as a mighty war-whoop, they "make up for a run." Goats, sheep, pigs, fowls, mammies scatter in all directions. The latter display lovely sets of teeth, and laugh heartily over the temporary panic.

The Fort at Anamabu is famous as having witnessed the first visit of the Ashanti army to a coast town. This was in 1807, when the king in person led twenty thousand warriors to battle. The Fort was bravely defended by a handful of English and native officers and men from the attacks of Sai Tootoo Quamina. His Majesty declared that he had only come to the Coast to look for a runaway chief, who had added injury to insult by killing some of his, the king's, messengers. It was felt, however, that if the experiment with the walls of Anamabu had succeeded from a military standpoint, Sai Tootoo Quamina might have gone to look for some one else at the Capital—Cape Coast Castle. The Governor at the latter place had so much respect for Ashanti that he set to work and secured the person of the runaway chief, who had fled to the town for protection, and handed him over to Sai Tootoo Quamina to be hacked in pieces. As the Ashantis were unpopular with the Fantis generally, the natives of Anamabu had espoused the cause of the fugitive chief; but when overpowered by the superior forces, skill, and courage of Ashanti they fled, some to their fishing canoes and others, about 1,500, to the Fort. As the siege continued and as numbers of the natives were dying, the Cape Coast Governor yielded to the demands of Sai Tootoo, and handed half of the refugees over to his Majesty, who immediately sold them into slavery.[1] The other half were claimed by the Governor and his colleagues, and also sold! Happily

[1] In the palmy days of the slave trade it was not an unusual sight to see between twenty and thirty ships of sail, of different nations, waiting at Anamabu for consignments of slaves; though permitted by law to carry only five hundred on a voyage, sometimes as many as seven hundred would be closely packed into a ship; they were branded in order to ensure identity. Gold coast slaves realised better prices than did those from other parts of the coast; many committed suicide by drowning, others by deliberate starvation.

there was at least one humane Englishman in the Colony at the time. Mr. John Swanzy, the Governor of Accra, hearing of the truculent conduct of his fellow-countrymen at Cape Coast, rose from his sick bed and took boat for the Capital and poured out vials of wrath upon the council, with the result that the unhappy slaves who had not actually left the roadstead for the West Indies were permitted to return to their town. The effort cost the brave man his life. He returned to Accra, and died shortly afterwards.

But to return to our journey. My work really began at Mankessim, which I reached in the afternoon of the second day. As we regard it our duty to teach our people to "honour the king," I called upon his Majesty of Mankessim. From him I gathered traditionary information respecting the history of his people. I think I may venture to repeat it, for it was given in the presence of the principal officers of state, and was confirmed by sundry grunts of approval on all sides. "Mankessim is the oldest Fanti kingdom. When the Fantis came from Takyiman they halted in that neighbourhood preparatory to branching out in various directions and forming minor kingdoms. The great yearly council, however, was held at Mankessim, whose king naturally presided. At these gatherings matters affecting the whole Fanti community were considered. Criminals under sentence of death were taken to the old capital, and were executed by spear, or knife, or gun. Occasionally victims for sacrifice were buried alive. When the Fantis paid their visit to the place they acknowledged as their chief idol one which was known as Nanaam." It was interesting to note what the stately old king Kweku Mbill said concerning the superstition of his ancestors, and his thankfulness that the Gospel light was penetrating the dark places of his kingdom. The king's silver-headed sceptre bore the following inscription—

"DOOR DENDIRECTEUR GENERAAL
JOAN VAN SEVENTWYSEM IS DESEM
VEREERT AAN APREDIMGUE PRAFFO
VAN FANTUM AD 1701."

Sunday was a busy day; Divine Service at 8 o'clock, Sunday School at 11.30. The latter part of the school hour was devoted to theological questions and answers; but the usual order of things was reversed. One and another of the adult scholars put interesting questions to the missionary, which led to profitable conversation. At the afternoon service the Sacrament of Baptism was administered to a young man who expressed an intelligent belief in the Articles of the Christian faith, and also to two infants. The king attended service in our chapel, and accompanied us to a meeting held in the open air. I observed that my faithful cook took a seat amongst the aristocracy of the place. At the evening service the Sacrament of the Lord's Supper was administered.

Before we left Mankessim our people brought presents of oranges, yams and fowls. His Majesty sent a kingly present in the shape of a magnificent ram; and I was also made the happy possessor of a famous bush hat.

As I have already stated my belief that Fetishism is disappearing, I feel that I must here make mention of the marvellous victory of Christianity over the pagan religion in Mankessim. Just as the kingdom is the oldest in the Fanti country, so the Fetish priests regarded Mankessim as the headquarters of their power. Fifty years ago five priests ministered at the altars of the great Fetish. It would be wearisome to follow these tricksters through all their chicanery and jugglery with which they duped their people. Not only were converts to Christianity led to understand the nature of the impostures, but heathen chiefs expressed their disgust at the deception. While lust was reigning supreme at the orgies, human victims were offered in sacrifice. And when, at length, the strong arm of the Government intervened to put a stop to bloodshed, the priests arranged for crowds of their followers to surround the groves, and by their unearthly yells to drown the screams of the victims of superstition. Truly a work of grace was needed to enable the first Christian disciples to convert those bloody groves into a farm, and to build a church near the old Fetish house now in ruins. To God be all the praise!

Next morning, November 5th, we were early astir, and left for Abassa. In crossing over a river I was greatly pleased to learn that practical consideration is shown to Christian missionaries by the heathen who derive a part of their income from the toll levied at the ferry. A sum of threepence is collected from each passenger conveyed in the canoe. It is generally understood that the sums thus collected are periodically divided between the king, the inhabitants of the neighbouring town, and the ferryman. I have seen Mr. Bushman endeavour, but without success, to elude the vigilant eye of the collector, and I have also seen those who did not choose to pay swim the river; but I have never seen the ferryman who demanded toll of the missionary. This is a consideration, particularly when the missionary has such a number of carriers, who are also allowed a free passage. This generous recognition obtains in all parts of the Colony. Of course there is the inevitable "dash": but then the average native would almost rather die than forgo the pleasure of receiving that. Love for "dash" seems to be bred in the bone.

At Abassa I had the pleasure of meeting a catechist with a face as black as coal, but with a heart as free from guile as that of any man—black or white—that I have met in Africa. My good friend was "passing rich on £20 a year." I suppose he was the only "scholar" in that town, but he wielded a mighty influence upon all with whom he came into contact. He was the friend and counsellor of kings and chiefs, and was held in the highest esteem among all men in the villages for many miles round. To such as he, representatives of all ranks of society come to have their domestic, social, and political grievances adjusted. How beautiful in its simplicity is the following extract from his "minute" book, which, I may parenthetically remark, was certainly not written for my information, but was, at my suggestion, very readily placed at my disposal. "Business of local preachers' meeting." (1) "I put before the meeting if any of us know something against his neighbour on behalf of his preaching, his moral character, or anything against Christianity, you must put out the said man: if nothing, lift up your hands. We all lift up our hands, as we know nothing against any of us." (2) "Theological exercises." I have hinted that the catechist was the only scholar in the place: so that it becomes part of his duty to instruct the less favoured local preachers in order that they may preach to others. I have elsewhere stated that all natives are blessed with marvellously retentive memories:[1] hence the theological exercises. How attentively the illiterate brethren listen to their loved teacher as, with the aid of a six-

---

[1] I have been amazed at the ease with which a native reproduces sermons and addresses; and yet such feats should surprise no one, for, in the absence of writing materials, the diary, the account book, the family will have been recorded in the memory, which has thus had endless exercise.

penny-halfpenny lamp, he reads and translates a passage of Scripture or unfolds what is to them some new and important truth. Attention is also given to Methodist doctrine. We have seen above what care is taken to guard against heterodox teaching. (3) "I suggest to the meeting how we shall manage for the reviving of our three stations. —— proposes that we visit the sick and weak members once a Sunday from house to house. I also propose to make three band meetings and *vangelize*. The meeting agree to the proposal." Subsequent paragraphs inform us that on a given Sunday a series of meetings were held. They began in the dewy morn at 4 o'clock, and were continued till chilly eve at 11 o'clock. The results of these special meetings called forth the gratitude of our humble friends. "The whole congregation dismissed on the next day after morning prayer with comfortable address of departure, St. Mark v. 19, by myself." But business relating to the material building was attended to. "I suggest to the meeting to set a time to cut the thatches for the roofing of the chapel. . . . we also consider the moneys collected for the chapel, and we found £7 4s.: it is with —— and some is with ——, which she promised to produce the papers to see the accounts on to-morrow, to see so much is with her."

At this place we had a large congregation. Our company included Mohammedans as well as pagans. My faithful cook informed me that —— had interpreted "berry nicely." "Oh, indeed! what did he say?" "De same as you did, sah!" "Well, what did I say?" Then the cook's mouth opened, as some would say, from ear to ear, as he grinned and confessed that he had quite forgotten. Evidently he thought I was too particular.

How the heart ached at the thought of the low moral standard of those who were emerging from heathenism! But then the greatest missionary that the world has ever seen, when dealing with a people infinitely superior intellectually to the African, had far more trying experiences. We read that he found it necessary to exhort the "fellow-citizens with the saints and of the household of God" to "put away lying and stealing." There were members of other Churches whose shameful conduct greatly distressed St. Paul. The Apostle's experience teaches us to exercise more patience towards those who, deeply sunk in sin, have but an imperfect knowledge of "the first principles of the doctrine of Christ."

Here I had to deal with the offence of a man who had taken to himself a second wife on the ground that his first wife had become disfigured by disease, and, moreover, was useless in attending to her household duties. The plea of the offender was, that as he had paid a sum of money and gifts to the parents and friends of the wife, he was perfectly justified in doing what he liked with his own.

Instances somewhat similar to this might be given to show that our methods must be on the principle of "line upon line .... precept upon precept." A somewhat amusing case came under notice. A male member of the Church was engaged with his brethren in re-roofing the chapel. His wife, with other ladies, had "gone to bush," to cut grass to serve as thatch. It seems that the good lady tarried longer than was absolutely necessary, for her husband went in search of her, and found her gossiping with a sister who had brought trouble into the otherwise peaceful domestic circle through her love for tattle. The lord and master was enraged, and rated the gossip all the way back to the chapel, much to the amusement, it was said, of the heathen. The aggrieved sister charged the offender at the ecclesiastical court, and he was asked to apologise. This he refused to do. The members of the court then called in councillors from adjoining villages, when the extraordinary decision was arrived at, that the brother should not only apologise but pay a shilling to the offended sister! As he continued refractory, I was asked to uphold the decision of the court. Of course I explained that that was not in my power; but I succeeded in inducing the brother to express regret for having brought ridicule upon the woman and upon his religion. At the suggestion of the thoughtful catechist it was decided that as a public scandal had been created, the expression of regret should be proclaimed in the chapel on the following Sunday morning.

On the morning of my departure from the town I called on the chief to thank him for practical help in re-thatching the chapel. Work of this kind is frequently undertaken by heathens as well as Christians. I also desired the old man to exercise greater influence in keeping his unruly heathen subjects from molesting the Christians and interrupting their services. The chief complained that the influence and authority of chiefs had been considerably weakened by the Government. I admitted that that was so, but pointed out that the Government was at all times prepared to support chiefs in their attempt to keep order, and I further hinted that incapable chiefs were sometimes removed from their exalted positions.

The journey to Gyirankuma was performed on foot, for the path was decidedly too narrow to admit of the passage of the hammock. Screened from the sun by the dense bush and giant trees, how indescribably grand was that walk. In the forest at daybreak one becomes conscious of the almost simultaneous awakening of nature; in a few moments everything seems instinct with life and vigour. One feels that before any adequate conception of the grandeur of African scenery can be conveyed, new words and similes must be added to the language, and new colours to the palette.

It is not so much a difference in degree as in kind. The feeling is that "no words can work up the fancy," and that " typographical attempts to move the imagination will be of no use." It is not so much that the scene is sublime or charming, as grand and majestic. The feelings produced are not rapturous or ecstatic, but rather those of awe and dread. Towering above trees whose form would grace an English forest, were the stately trees of commerce, and higher still those of more rapid growth and consequently softer nature. "Higher still is the waving surface of an ocean of foliage .... a vast sea of tree-tops, whose waves ripple in a region seemingly set between earth and heaven." Below is a tangled mass of vegetable life struggling for existence and supremacy, yet rising superior to a dense undergrowth. Here mangrove and cactus, reed and sedge, thorn and briar, huddled together in the wildest profusion, and flourished above mud and water; while[1] "matted and tangled creepers hung in heavy festoons from the lofty branches, and clung to the dense undergrowth beneath." The sun was beating with all his fury somewhere above, but not into the heart of that forest; no fierce ray penetrated that region. Vast numbers of gaudy butterflies sprang from the trees. Birds of every conceivable plumage disported themselves in quest of their early meal. The forest seemed full of life; so numerous and varied were the sounds, colours, and motions

[1] Major W. F. Butler's *Akim Foo.*

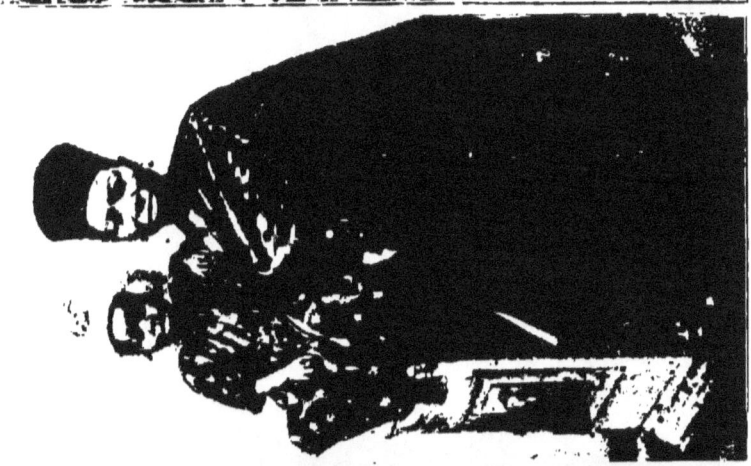

TYPES OF NATIVE DRESS.

To face page 80.

of the indescribable insects, birds, and beasts that inhabited this region.

I do not know that I need repeat the programme of the several days' experience. The object of my visit was to strengthen the hands of the Catechists, to endeavour to utter words of counsel, of encouragement or reproof, as circumstances required, to our congregations; to administer the Sacraments, and to investigate cases of discipline. Occasionally it was necessary to appear exceedingly stern in reproving cant, hypocrisy, and notorious sin. But one was always prepared to make allowances for surroundings, and one never really felt quite all that one's manner might have indicated.

The missionary certainly has his times of depression, both when travelling in the interior as well as when on the seaboard. But there are corresponding compensations. My friend Hall relates the following, as having occurred in the neighbourhood of Gyirankuma. "A woman, old and diseased, told us, with tears, how through the abandonment by her husband, who had taken younger women as wives, she was on the point of committing suicide, for the purpose of bringing punishment upon him, when she was attracted by the singing band and was influenced to join the Christian people. Shortly afterwards she was converted; she then asked her new friends to help her with her prayers for the conversion of her husband. United prayers resulted in reunited lives; husband and wife were again happy in the love of one another. The old woman wished to acknowledge God's goodness."

From what has been seen at Abassa, it will be easily understood that education makes little headway in the interior schools. Indeed, the "Bush" natives have entertained decided objections to day-schools, on the ground that their youths, when educated, leave for the Coast towns, and take situations in the Government and Mercantile Services. Special attention has therefore been given by the native ministers to industrial training, such as plantation work, with encouraging results. One youth, while passing through a truly rural school, attempted to improve some lines which are familiar to most of us, and produced the following :—

> "I am chief of any I can see,
> My write there is no one to correct,
> From the middle all round to the ocean
> I am chief of the cock and the goat;
> Oh solitude (death) where are thy health
> Yon sages have seen in your face?
> Better dwell in the centre of colds
> Than reign in this restless land."

In the course of my journey I had the pleasure of meeting the Reverend J. O. Hammond, Mr. Hall's native colleague. This minister's love for work is proverbial, and he is famous in the district for neatness in keeping his circuit accounts. I venture to repeat the particulars of an incident brought to our notice by the native minister about this time. A man, who had been a prominent member of our church in the neighbourhood of Salt Pond, relapsed into Mohammedanism. He then became a vigorous opponent of our work, even to the length of holding open-air meetings, in order to attack our Mission, and to induce our people to embrace Islam. While lying on his death-bed he soon became filled with remorse, on account of his backsliding. "My wife, children and I have resolved to become Christians, I beg you to give us back our names," in other words, that their names might be re-entered on our Church Roll. "Why," replied the minister, "there is but one God, who is the God of Mohammedans and Christians alike. Why leave the crescent for the cross?" "Ah," said the man, "I have known what it is to be a Christian. I once felt the hopes and joys of the Christian faith. Since my backsliding I have had no peace of conscience. Once I could be happy without a penny, but I have gained nothing by desertion to Islam, but doubt of heaven and fear of hell. Give us back our names! I have put away my strange wife, and have only the one to whom I was first married, who is also sick, and anxious to serve Christ. Give us back our names." He afterwards died in hope, but the influence of his death so affected one of his comrades as to cause him, too, to forsake the crescent for the cross. I have been reminded by this story of a conversation I once had with a European surgeon at Cape Coast, who suggested that it was necessary to charge our discourses with brimstone to make them effective. I said then what I say now, emphatically, *never*. And, if I know anything of the methods of my European and Native colleagues, I say the same of their sermons and addresses. Not that our eschatology was in the least degree open to question from the orthodox point of view, or that we deliberately ignored unpopular subjects, but we felt that we had a more excellent way of leading men to acknowledge God as their Father, Christ as their Saviour, the Holy Ghost as their Comforter. If our audiences were more enlightened, and we had a suspicion that there was open defiance of the Divine Commands, we should possibly be more severe.

But I have digressed! My tour occupied ten days. On the return journey I walked a great part of the distance, and once was far ahead of my carriers. The cook was under the impression that there was an unwillingness on the part of the men to carry me, accordingly he "read the articles of war." "I go make palaver wid dem hammock-men fo' make my master walk. My master get sick!" Honest, faithful old Dondoh! How deeply we regretted his illness and death a few years later.

The "pastoral visitation" was, as I have said, an education to myself; and, I trust, was of service to the various workers and congregations. The friends everywhere were very kind. It may perhaps be of interest to the reader to know the variety in food at the two principal meals of the day. At the town of Salt Pond I was made welcome at the table of Europeans, where a feast of fat things was provided. But when left to our own resources in the Bush it was otherwise. The first meal consisted of yam, rice, and chicken, the next, by way of a change, of chicken, rice, and yam; the third of rice, yam, and chicken, and so on until we returned to Cape Coast and Civilisation.

CHAPTER VI

RELATES CIRCUMSTANCES WHICH WILL SUMMON AN IMMENSE CONCOURSE OF PEOPLE—A FUNERAL, A FIRE, OR A FESTIVAL; AND HAS A REFERENCE TO ELMINA CASTLE AND ITS CONNECTION WITH THE ASHANTI WAR OF 1873, AND CONCLUDES WITH REMARKS RESPECTING PERSONAL ASSOCIATES

AT the end of my first wet season one of the leading members of Cape Coast Society died, and I was asked to conduct the funeral service. I was greatly surprised to find that the corpse was enclosed in a most elaborate brass-covered coffin, which was conveyed to the cemetery in a plumed hearse and followed by an enormous concourse of people. Although interments usually take place between twelve and eighteen hours after death,[1] there is not the slightest difficulty in securing an attendance of some thousand or fifteen hundred followers, for the news spreads like wildfire. Good Templars, Oddfellows, Freemasons, Volunteers, as occasion requires, all turn out in full regalia to swell the ranks. When such an event occurs there is no lack of mourning. In addition to the sorrow of the bereaved friends, there is the dismal lamentation of those who can

[1] I have been requested, when on a journey, to conduct a funeral service over the body of a child two hours after death.

command tears at a moment's notice.¹ In interior towns and villages, even more than at Cape Coast, is observed the ancient custom of the "mourners going about the streets." In Christian homes it is usual to invite friends to the house to join in singing hymns during the night. Although coffee and biscuits are provided on these occasions, our scholars have, nevertheless, worn a very jaded appearance as they have presented themselves at school the morning following a wake—sleepy and hoarse with the exertions of the night. This solace might prove too great a strain for the nerves of European friends, but it certainly is greatly in advance of the pagan custom of spending the night in drinking spirits and beating tom-toms.²

[1] At the interment of a West Indian soldier, a comrade burst into tears, for no other reason than that a little water was seen at the bottom of the grave.

[2] The funeral customs of the pagans of Abassa are as follows: During the first three days rum is imbibed very freely; three weeks later the drinking is repeated; after the lapse of six weeks, and before the expiration of twelve months, guns are fired, and there is a general beating of tom-toms, followed by a great feast. At all these feasts a chair, covered with a white sheet, occupies a prominent position; upon this chair is placed a plate, and upon the plate is poured a libation; money and food are also placed thereon, in order that the spirit may eat and drink with the guests, and keep them in health, and heal them of their diseases.

Less than thirty years ago it was the custom that when two men quarrelled, and one as a result committed suicide, the other was made to follow his example. Instances of supposed witchcraft were occasionally tried. The corpse of one said to have been bewitched was borne by men who, at a spot previously arranged, would begin to stagger. Usually this was done near a house, in which case the bearers would run round the house several times, and finally shoot the corpse through a window, and bring out the owner to certain death.

Making mention of the concourse of people brings to remembrance the vision of a multitude which no man could number, that assembled in our compound between the hours of one and three one eventful morning. Our kitchen, which was built of wood, had caught fire. The flames attracted the attention of a nurse at the military hospital, who very quickly aroused me from my slumber; and soon a small crowd gathered. It was so evident that nothing could save the unfortunate kitchen that, with the assistance of my military friend, I cut off the connection between the flames and the house, thankful for the thought that no more serious mischief could be done. But the small crowd mentioned above seemed to think that I did not sufficiently realise the gravity of the situation, and then and there it was decided to act seriously. The first business was to collect a bigger crowd. Accordingly one of the number went for the school bell, and rang it with all his might. Another bolted off to "Wesley" and rang the church bell, another fled for the auctioneer's bell, and another thought of that execrable pagan horn and blew a blast too awful for words; and still another thought of the tom-tom, and in about twenty minutes we had a most perfect pandemonium. Out of the thousands thus drawn together no fewer than twenty-seven persons actually worked, twenty women, six men and a boy. The women fetched the water; five men and the boy poured the water on the flames; the sixth man took a pickaxe and industriously pulled down some brick pedestals which he evidently thought were in danger of igniting.

There are memories of other crowds. Christmas appears to be the greatest festival of the year. It is usual, wherever practicable, to have the "spring cleaning" over in anticipation of the season. The new whitewash and paint show to great advantage in the blazing sun, for it is the driest, and therefore the hottest, part of the year. Not only are buildings renovated but wardrobes are replenished; new suits of clothes are donned; little people, for the first time in their experience, hobble about the town in tight-fitting boots and shoes, and there is general rejoicing for a week or ten days. The proprietor of the merry-go-round reaps a rich harvest; for, in addition to the entrance fee of sixpence to witness the wonderful sight, a further sum is collected from those who are equal to a circular ride. At this festal season heathen as well as Christians rejoice. Nights are made hideous by the horn-blowing and tom-tomming of the patriots, and one is reminded of a remark that was once made anent a performance of a Siamese band: "If I were their king, I'd hang the men and burn their instruments!" But being of a milder temperament you vehemently express the wish merely that the instruments were at the bottom of the sea. The noise of the more civilised brass instruments is scarcely less tormenting; you can only long for the morning. Such a commotion was there during the season of 1888 that it was necessary to turn out the garrison to restore order and to patrol the town.

We have now reached the end of our first year at Cape Coast. It is much too early to speak of progress, but I cannot resist the temptation to say that at this time our day school passed a very creditable examination by H. M. Inspector, at 97 per cent. On one of my visits to the school I found that the senior lads had written an article on kanky—the staple food of the natives. We were told from what it was made, how it was made, and all the rest of it, in a very intelligent manner. One boy added : " But I do not like kanky ; and were it not that children are taught to obey their parents in all things, I should refuse to eat it ! "

The Sunday Schools continued to flourish, and, according to the testimony of native friends, to exert an influence for good in the homes of the people. The following will be interesting as a specimen of a Fanti hymn : it is an exhortation to praise God.

> [1] " Mu sunsum nsueri yi Nyami ayew ;
> Mu sunsum nsueri yin' ayew ;
> Nyhira onka Nyankupon nyi ni Ba ;
> Ndasi onka Nyankupon nyi ni Ba ;
> Ayeyi onka Nyankupon nyi ni Ba ;
> Na, mu sunsum, nsueri yin' ayew."

---

[1] " Arise, my soul, and praise the Lord ;
Arise, my soul, and praise Him ;
Let blessings be upon God and His Son ;
Let thanks be given to God and His Son ;
Let praise be ascribed to God and His Son ;
Arise, my soul and praise Him."

The Harmattan paid its annual visit to us at the opening of the new year. This wind, which blows from Central Africa towards the Atlantic, is cool in the early morning, but warm in the middle of the day. It is said that fine particles of dust are brought by it from the Sahara. We certainly found it most difficult to keep the house free from dust at this season. A great feature of the Harmattan is that it is a health-bringing wind; but when you suddenly trip against your floor-cloth, which has taken to curling, and you find the covers of your books in all sorts of shapes, while the Madeira furniture is incessantly creaking—well, you involuntarily confess that you would sacrifice a degree or two of health, if only you could get things straight. But the visitor soon takes its departure, and comparative order is restored. Tornadoes may be expected in March, and heavy rains at any time between that month and July. Lighter rains follow, and the natives tell us that the white man may renew the lease of his life on the 25th of September (!) (While writing I have been reminded of the sight of a colleague in his rain coat, preparing to collect fresh water, in various receptacles, as it fell through the ceiling of his dining-room. I think also of another who, on returning from a journey, had the pleasure of beholding the corrugated iron roof of his house deposited in his compound by a tornado. I have myself been grateful for the friendly shelter of an umbrella when retiring to rest for the night.)

It need scarcely be said that travelling is undertaken, as far as practicable, in the dry season. Hence it was that I went on a tour to Axim in February. The journey was much longer than the one already described. I need not give any particulars, for the work was practically the same as that in the Anamabu District, except that less attention was given to pastoral work, and more time was devoted to the schools, which sorely needed re-organisation; everything was being done in a most slipshod fashion.

A great part of the road was by the sea-shore, which, when the tide was out, gave us a solid path, but which at other times was most wearying. Great kindness was shown to us by the representatives of the trading houses of Messrs. F. & A. Swanzy of Cannon Street, who have factories at the principal towns along the Coast.

Elmina Castle lay in our way. As no particular reference has been made to this historic building, it may be worth while to mention that it is the oldest and most substantial fort in the Colony, or indeed in any part of West Africa. It was built in 1481 by direction of King John the Second of Portugal. At that time the Englishmen prepared to fit out a fleet for the coast of Guinea.[1] "Hearing of their preparations King John at once sent an embassy to England to remonstrate, and, so great was the

---

[1] *Historical Geography of British Colonies, West Africa.* Lucas, Clarendon Press.

name of Portugal at the time, so strong the respect for the Papal Bull of 1442, by which the Portuguese discoveries were safeguarded, that the English King, Edward the Fourth, agreed to the demand that the fleet should be dissolved, and the expedition given up." But the Portuguese monopoly of the African trade soon proved irritating not only to the English, but to the Dutch and the French, and representatives of these nations decided to claim a share of the spoils. But although they looked with envious eyes upon the rich possessions they hesitated for a time to enter into conflict with the powerful owners. The Dutch, however, eventually decided to make an attempt, and in 1624 they built Fort Nassau, to the east of Cape Coast, to which reference has already been made, and thirteen years later, with the assistance of a formidable fleet they took possession of the castle of St. George.

In 1867 the Dutch, after incurring enormous cost in the maintenance of their forts, agreed to cede to the English all forts to the east of Elmina in exchange for the forts of the English to the west of Cape Coast. This partition proved an immense advantage to the English, who were by far the most popular rulers of the coast tribes, and a correspondingly great disadvantage to the Dutch, who experienced endless trouble with the natives, in holding their new possessions. Hence it came to pass that the Dutch were thankful to hand over to the English the whole of their forts for the nominal value of the stores which they happened to have on hand. A convention to this effect was signed at the Hague on February 25th, 1871. Six weeks later the British Governor of the West African settlements made his formal entry into Elmina. Thus it came to pass that, of the Portuguese, the Dutch, the Danes, the Brandenburghers, and the English, who had come to the Gold Coast seeking gold and slaves, the English alone were left.

But in taking over their new possessions the English experienced unforeseen (?) difficulties. The Ashanti kingdom, in exercising a powerful sway over the interior tribes, had been in the habit of receiving an annual sum from the Elmina Governor which the Dutch had given to the ruler of Denkera as a guarantee for their rent. The English had no inclination to continue the payment, and the Ashantis soon became aware of this. Added to the disappointment, the Ashantis learnt that, while the English were the avowed protectors of the coast and interior tribes, there was very little sympathy with their own nation. These facts led to the Ashanti war of 1873, the results of which are well known.

Fort St. George is now used partly as a residence for Government officers, and partly for the safe keeping of political prisoners. It was here that Prempeh of Kumasi and his chiefs were recently detained previous to their transference to Sierra Leone.

To turn from the historical to the personal.

In my first year I knew only two friends among my fellow-countrymen, apart from my colleague. This was partly due to the fact that I had little time for making or returning calls, and partly because I imagined that the majority of Europeans and I had little in common. Not that the two visitors just mentioned agreed with me upon all subjects, but both were decidedly entertaining. The one with High principles discoursed on the defects of my ecclesiasticism; and the other, an avowed agnostic, regarded it his duty to make general and sweeping charges against native Christians. I use the word *general*, because when I invited my friend to specify a charge, so that I might deal with it, he subsided. By the way, my friend had a servant—not a Christian—whom he nicknamed after one of our leading statesmen. I inquired the reason; for although the names of "Bottle-of-beer," "Glasgow," "Prince of Wales," "Blackman Trouble," and the like are common enough among Kru boys, I had never, in this connection, heard the name of this particular statesman. "Oh," said my friend, "the explanation is simple enough: the boy is such a *fearful liar!*" So that, according to the critic, the ultra-African-liar *can* be matched in England, even though it is necessary to appeal to Parliament. Seriously, my friend's estimate of the African character had as little weight with me as had his judgment respecting the character of the politician.

I am afraid that in those days I was somewhat of

a recluse. I observed that the majority of my fellow-countrymen were remarkable for their absence from church; I therefore concluded that there was no particular need to widen the circle of my acquaintances. In this I was greatly mistaken: for, while it must be admitted that there are those of our own colour whose companionship is not at all times particularly desirable, yet there are many whose friendship we have highly valued, whom we shall be happy to meet at any time. I may perhaps be permitted to say that friends in England have been more than interested in knowing that their sons, separated from them by thousands of miles of water, and exposed to great physical and moral danger, have made a friend of the missionary.

And now the time was hastening on when, in order to avoid a second wet season, I was to take my first furlough. This began in the middle of May. Just before leaving Cape Coast, a West Indian soldier called on me for a little spiritual advice and the loan of a few shillings. He had the former, but I am afraid it did not benefit him very much, for he did not get the latter. On reflection, though, I'm inclined to think he did get it: for I have a dim recollection that the man was ever after conspicuous by his absence, which is a bad sign. Yes, I'm afraid that I must regard it as a bad debt—the only one I ever contracted in Africa, by the way. My advice to the reader, whether residing in Africa or in England, is, if asked for a loan, and the application is prefaced by a few pious phrases, take warning from my inexperience.

À propos of money-lending, my Irish neighbour sent me his clerk, who had got into financial difficulties, and thence into the clutches of the money-lender, who demanded interest at the rate of 10 per cent. The account had been running for some time, and, although the principal had been repaid, the compound interest had run up to a similar amount. The law was set in motion, and the apparently unhappy clerk was in danger of being sold up. I was requested to intercede, but my zeal got the upper hand of my judgment. When I found that Shylock would not abate a farthing of the claim, I "delivered my soul." The result was such a letter! This document has a place in my cabinet of curiosities. No word of acknowledgment did I receive from the client, who went about his business as unconcernedly as possible. *Moral*: Do not interfere between the native money-lender and his client. The latter is certain to take very good care of himself.

And now for the return to England. One of the noblest characters I ever met in Africa was the gentleman whose cabin I shared on that voyage— the late Reverend J. Alfred Robinson, of the Niger Mission, Church Missionary Society. We held united services in the saloon, and spent hours together in Biblical study and in conversation respecting methods of work in Africa and the character of Christian converts. From those conversations one gathered that there was much that was depressing in the Mission work on the Niger. I was thankful to feel more hopeful concerning the Gold Coast. Mr. Robinson seemed to think that work in his district might be more successful if the workers adopted a simpler style of dress—or rather the national dress. This certainly might have been the case on the Niger, particularly among the Mohammedans of the upper parts of the river; but I feel quite convinced that such methods at the Gold Coast would avail nothing.

Among valued letters in my possession, I prize highly that from our departed friend. Surely his devotion to the work he loved so dearly justified the adoption of his motto for West Africa:

τὸ ζῆν Χρίστος
τὸ αποθανεῖν κέρδος.

CHAPTER VII

THE ARRIVAL OF THE ROMAN CATHOLIC MISSIONARIES AT CAPE COAST—THEOLOGICAL DIFFERENCES DO NOT AFFECT PERSONAL FRIENDSHIPS—THE REVEREND T. J. PRICE AND HIS DIFFICULTIES WITH THE VERNACULAR—HIS EXCELLENCY SIR W. BRANDFORD GRIFFITH, K.C.M.G.—HAPPY RELATIONS WITH ANGLICAN CLERGY

ON returning to Cape Coast five months later we were welcomed by our school assistants with the information that the Roman Catholic Missionaries of Elmina had proposed extending their work by opening, or, indeed, had actually opened, a school near our headquarters. Horror was writ large upon the faces of our informants. I think I said something to the effect that I did not care two straws about the "invasion." Certainly I felt that if the new Missionaries were bent only on benefiting the natives, so much the better for the latter; but if, as it was hinted, they were concerned only about upsetting our work they would find that we were not so easily moved. I will not anticipate our relations, always the happiest, with the nuns, until I write of Mrs. Kemp's arrival on the scene; except to say that our presents of oranges, of which we had a great quantity, were most graciously accepted by our late friend the saintly Sister Ignatius (?), one of the many whose lives have been sacrificed for the salvation of Africa.

With the sterner sex we were personally on the most friendly terms. What different nationalities were represented by the Roman Catholic Mission! True, there were no Englishmen among the number, but I remember Irish, Irish-American, French, Swiss, Alsatian, German, Canadian, and Dutch. Our native converts could not understand that I, a stout Protestant, could receive visits from the priests, and return their social calls. They have yet to learn that ecclesiastical differences need not necessarily affect personal friendship. I once ventured to ask one of the fraternity how it came to pass that their Missions generally were only established in those centres which we had held for half a century, while the purely heathen centres were allowed to remain untouched. I ventured to suggest that the introduction of a totally distinct Christian religion might prove bewildering to those who were just emerging from heathenism. The reply was, "The Roman Catholic Church recognises no other Church." "But you told me the other day that you thought I was a *good man.*" "Yes, but then you are *quite an exception to those of your faith.*" Now, what could you possibly do with one who was so lavish with his compliments? On another occasion Father—— remarked, "I understand that your colleague, Mr.—— will not allow his people to send their children to our school. I felt I must report the matter to you." My reply was: "Mr.—— has no alternative. Our Synod has decided that thus it must be, and I heartily concur. Protestant though I am, I am prepared to admit that I would infinitely rather that pagans should embrace your faith than remain as they are. But if our people decide that Protestant teaching is preferable for themselves, they certainly must decide the same for their young children." The legislation referred to was a severe but wholesome test of the faithfulness of our people. For in all our central schools we insist on the payment of school-fees; indeed all our important schools are self-supporting. Our rivals, on the other hand, give free education.

The reader who is familiar with the accounts of Paton's work in the New Hebrides, and of Mackay's work in Uganda, will understand the kind of difficulty that is experienced when Romanist Missionaries cross the path of the Protestant.

We were greatly cheered at the end of the year by receiving a communication from the medical attendant of the Gie Appantoo Gold Mining Company at Prestea—a hundred miles from Cape Coast —to the effect that he had established a school in the village. The Company, with Mr. Samuel Causton as chairman, had taken a great interest in the spiritual welfare of their employés, and also of the population of the immediate neighbourhood.

But Dr. Martin's undertaking was purely his own private venture. On leaving for England shortly afterwards he generously sent £40 to the Society as a proof of his wish to see the work continued. The floating nature of the population and lack of suitable workers account for the comparative failure of our work. But we are not without hope of permanent benefit arising from this undertaking—although at present it is one of the least satisfactory stations in the district.

Our forces were at this time strengthened by the presence of an old college friend, the Reverend T. J. Price, who was appointed to Accra—the seat of Government. The first few months, however, were spent at Cape Coast and Anamabu, gaining experience, and rendering valuable help in our schools. Occasionally Mr. Price was prostrated by fever. With one exception these attacks were of the mildest type, and I was able to deal with them without calling in medical aid. But in the last and most troublesome attack we happened to have a medical friend visiting us who had had but little experience of malarial fevers. The obstinacy of the attack and the method of treatment suggested the advisability of sending for our old friend, the surgeon attached to the garrison, and Mr. Price was soon himself. Malarial fevers are exceedingly difficult to diagnose. It is generally considered that laymen of experience in these fevers have a decided advantage over skilled surgeons, who lack practical experience. But the most skilled and the most painstaking surgeons, notwithstanding their long and varied experience, are at times completely baffled.

I have referred to Mr. Hall as a model organiser. Mr. Price excelled as a pastor. He was held in the highest esteem by his people, to whom he was devotedly attached. There were times when the plainness of his speech gave offence to offenders. But then there was no alternative, glaring sin needed reproof even at the risk of wounding the susceptibilities of those who sinned. I have to state this, for I wish to add that during his residence in our Colony, no Missionary was so generally beloved as was the Superintendent of our Accra Mission.

During the early months of his residence with me at Cape Coast, Mr. Price devoted some time to the study of the Fanti language, and as he had an aptitude for the study, he made considerable progress. But even he had difficulties at times, as the following extract from a letter will show :—

"On my arrival (at Legu) I was invited to about the only two-storied house in the village, where, on looking out of the upper story, I became a source of unspeakable interest and attraction to the villagers, who proceeded to discuss my personal appearance, the probable cost of my clothes, &c. While thus submitting myself, I sent for the catechist and told him I intended to hold a lantern-service, and that he would have to interpret. He begged to be excused, saying, he did not perfectly understand English. I urged him to make the attempt: it was useless. I thought I might, in this moment of sore need, turn to my faithful cook and general factotum, but again was disappointed. There was no alternative but to be independent and speak to my audience in Fanti. I must say that I was not entirely without confidence in my linguistic ability. We managed the opening ceremonies all right. I showed my pictures and began to speak in my best classical Fanti. Alas, some people have no taste for classic speech. Soon I heard ominous mutterings and shufflings. I paused and inquired if the audience could not hear. 'Oh yes!' was the reply, 'we can hear splendidly, but unfortunately we cannot understand a word you say. Will you kindly ask some one to interpret your address for you!' My unwilling cook was therefore pressed into the service.'

This experience reminds me of the fact that on one of my voyages to Africa, two military officers who were on their way to Grand Canary for the benefit of their health, went ashore at Teneriffe and asked in Spanish, as they imagined, for some cigars. The Spaniard appeared somewhat bewildered, and after a moment's pause replied in excellent English: "If you please, gentlemen, we do not speak *German* here!"

At the Synod of February, 1890, it was unanimously decided to appoint me to the oversight of the Aburah and Assin circuit, which stretches from within a few miles of Cape Coast to Prahsu, about midway between the former place and Kumasi. I very readily consented, for I was most anxious to be brought more directly into contact with the work which this new appointment involved. Moreover, I anticipated with no ordinary pleasure the prospect of meeting with our Christians of the interior.

At the same Synod it was also decided to allot different sections of the district to the European missionaries for the purpose of superintending the day schools. Our own school at Cape Coast increased in numbers, notwithstanding the fact that there were the important free schools of the Government and the Roman Catholic Mission near us. My first work in the Aburah circuit was to take a lad to Dunkwa to strengthen the teaching staff of the school. Dunkwa, by the way, is referred to by Hutton in his *Voyage to Africa*, 1820, under the name of Paintrey, and is recommended by him as a desirable place for the establishment of a school, in accordance with the wishes of the Earl of Bathurst, Secretary of State for the Colonies. My young friend set out in life amply stocked with clothing, a dozen books, two loaves of bread, three pennyworth of loaf sugar, and a small sum of money presented by various friends. But although his outfit was most modest, he rendered good service in the school and was highly esteemed by young and old alike at Dunkwa.

I had once again the pleasure of meeting the Rev. J. Alfred Robinson, who was returning to his work at the Niger in company with Mr. Wilmot Brooke and a strong party of Church Missionary Society Missionaries. Bishop Crowther was among them. The two young and zealous workers shortly afterwards entered into rest, soon to be joined by the saintly veteran. The policy adopted by the leaders of this party in carrying out much-needed reforms at the Niger Mission has been questioned. It certainly is just possible that had they but allowed themselves a rather longer period in which to accomplish all that they desired, their work might have been more effective. I have hesitated to say so much, for I feel that no more devoted or self-denying Missionaries ever visited Africa than Messrs. Robinson and Wilmot Brooke.

Dr. Battersby, who was on his way to the same district, gave me the pleasure of his company at Cape Coast for a week. We were very thankful for his services on the Sunday and also with the lads of our school during the week, and I had reason to believe that he was pleased with the results of our Missionary work at our headquarters.

I take this opportunity of saying that our relations with the Anglican chaplains of the Colony were of the most friendly nature. In England, where one is oftentimes tempted to imagine that the

VII A HEARTY RECEPTION FOR THE GOVERNOR

Anglican regards the Free Churchman with suspicion, and the Free Churchman regards the Anglican with jealousy, it is most refreshing to think of the times when Anglican and Wesleyan were positively cordial.

In the early part of May His Excellency the Governor, Sir W. B. Griffith, K.C.M.G., paid a visit to Cape Coast. There was a general desire to give him a hearty African reception. Accordingly some four or five thousand dusky subjects, with about a dozen Europeans, assembled on the most convenient open space in the town to give a lusty cheer. School children sang the National Anthem, pagans and Mohammedans beat their tom-toms with all the strength they possessed, and the noise was simply deafening. It was expected that His Excellency would make promises of improvements, which certainly were greatly needed in the town. But with the tact of a born diplomatist Sir Brandford refused to commit himself. He explained that, much as he loved Cape Coast, his hearers must bear in mind that he was a very-much-married Governor. He was wedded to all the towns, and that if he bestowed an undue share of affection upon the one with which he was then living, it would cause a good deal of unpleasantness among the other wives. At the conclusion of the ceremony His Excellency had a few kindly words to those about him. To the Missionary he expressed the wish to have all possible help in raising the morals of the rising generation, making an allusion to a glaring case of smuggling which had occurred a few months previously at Appam.

As I have observed from the newspaper the report of Sir Brandford Griffith's death I feel I must take this opportunity of offering a tribute of respect to his memory. While we never overlooked the fact that he was the Governor of the Colony, the representative of her Most Gracious Majesty the Queen, he always insisted that we should regard ourselves as the subjects of *paternal* government, and was always most sympathetic and kind in cases of sickness and suffering, down to the very humblest officer in the service.

Sir Brandford was a most pronounced Churchman, but he nevertheless was at all times prepared to render our Mission assistance from his private purse, and he repeatedly presided at our public meetings. It is needless to say that my relations with him were almost invariably of a purely official character, yet, nevertheless, I feel his death as that of a very true friend.

The wet season of 1890 was, residents said, the worst that had been known for seven years, though not as serious as that which followed five years later. But then our white population was comparatively small. Out of thirty, four died in two months, six were invalided away from the station, and the remainder, with one exception, were at various times laid aside; that exception was the surgeon, and he

THE LATE SIR W. BRANDFORD GRIFFITH, K.C.M.G., Lieutenant-Governor of the Gold Coast 1880 to 1887, Governor and Commander-in-Chief 1887 to 1895.

resembled a walking skeleton. This was the only occasion during the whole of my residence at the Gold Coast when I wondered—philosophically—who would be the next to "join the majority." Two of those taken from us were most advanced Ritualists; but ecclesiastical differences did not affect our friendship, and the friends in England were grateful for the attention shown by the Methodist missionary in the hour of need.

My second attack of fever was urged as a reason for taking a voyage to Accra—seventy miles to the east of Cape Coast. The vessel, fortunately, had several stoppages to make at the smaller ports, so that the three days on the good ship *Roquelle* restored me to my normal condition. It is a well-known fact that a change from one station to another, even though it is only a dozen miles away, is of the greatest benefit, except when the convalescent visits a place only to find that his fellow-countrymen are busily engaged burying their dead.

With returning health and strength it was found necessary to devote attention to the new school building. It was proposed to erect premises to accommodate three hundred scholars, at a cost of £440, including apparatus. The Government contributed one-eighth of this amount, friends in England added £45, but the remaining £340 was cheerfully subscribed by friends in the town. I must not forget to mention the readiness with which my fellow-countrymen in the Colonial service, as well as the Merchant, responded to the appeal,—notwithstanding the fact that at a tennis party an officer of the West Indian regiment complained that he could afford himself no refreshments, as he had that afternoon been visited by the missionary.

The mode of erecting a mud building may be of interest. The soil—or "swish" as it is locally known at Cape Coast—is decidedly granitic, and consequently exceedingly hard. The only preparation required is to mix the swish with water to the consistency of freshly-moulded bricks, make up into balls of half-a-dozen pounds weight, and lay courses of twelve or eighteen inches at intervals of three days. Our walls at the foundation were two feet three inches in thickness, above the floor twenty inches, and from the bottom of the window frames sixteen inches. The corners and centres of the walls were of fire-burnt bricks, and the whole was neatly plastered and whitewashed. The floor was composed of brick covered with a layer of cement. The massive pitch-pine doors, together with the roof, were made in England. We had to manipulate a solid pitch-pine girder measuring 20 feet, by 18 inches square for the support of folding doors, and to get that log "as true as a hair" eight feet above the floor, with only the assistance of my coloured workers, taxed my ingenuity, while at the same time I was in mortal fear that through some bungling they would let the whole thing collapse and make mince-meat of the careless labourers. But no accident occurred during the whole twelve months that "Wesley Centenary" was in course of erection. It has long since become far too small to meet the needs of our educational work.

CHAPTER VIII

RECORDS A MEMORABLE JOURNEY THROUGH ABURAH AND ASSIN, AND FURNISHES ILLUSTRATIONS OF THE FETISH PRIESTCRAFT

THE journey to Aburah and Assin in September was of great interest. Our first halting-place was at Ekroful; our hotel the Mission chapel. At the conclusion of the midday meal a deputation, consisting of the leaders of the Church, waited upon me to inform me that two years previously the whole village had been destroyed by fire, and that they were then engaged in re-building the house of the Catechist, but they needed funds. With considerable hesitancy they ventured to name the sum—£7. They had built the walls and fixed the roof. All that was now required was the services of a carpenter to make doors, windows, frames, and two tables; a bricklayer to plaster the walls, a quantity of lime, and the iron furniture for the joiner's use. The whole outlay would not exceed the sum mentioned. Small as it was I could only advance one half of the amount.

On approaching Dunkwa we passed a spring of water which, it was said, was greatly in requisition at the time of the Ashanti war of 1873. On the opposite side of the road a young damsel was most religiously going through her ablutionary exercises. Our cook remonstrated: the girl removed a few yards further away so that the essence of the soap should not find its way into the spring. I afterwards observed that the water poured into my filter was of the same soapy hue that I had observed at the spring, and was once more forced to the conclusion that, though the Fantis might claim to be clean in their persons, they were certainly most filthy in their habits.

But Sunday at Dunkwa proved a compensation for all the dirty water. The native Missionary in charge of this station informed me, with justifiable pride, that he had acted as an interpreter to Sir Archibald Alison during the Ashanti war. He ventured to suggest that his fellow-countrymen were most brave when led by English soldiers. But then the old patriot's ideas of bravery were very vague, for I happened to know that it was a notorious fact that the Fanti volunteers were on that occasion most cowardly.

The Reverend J. A. Graham had arranged for a lengthy day's services; he had invited the Christians from villages in the immediate neighbourhood to take part in these services, and, in order to screen them from the rays of the vertical sun, he had for some days previously been busily engaged with his school children and members of his congregation in extemporising a bamboo temple, the roof of which was formed of palm branches. The effect of the bright dresses of the congregation of some four or five hundred devout worshippers certainly was most picturesque. There were services at 4 a.m., 7 a.m., 9.30 a.m., 10.30 a.m., 12.30 p.m., 2 p.m., and 3 p.m. At the latter meeting the Christians were given the opportunity of testifying to their heathen neighbours the value of the Christian experience. I was greatly impressed with the experience of an aged chief, who informed us that he had been endeavouring to serve God for the last forty years. He also told us that many years previously a king of Elmina once desired his uncle to swear loyalty to him in view of a war that was then pending. The chief refused, but said, "Wait till the fight begins, and then you will see who are loyal!" The incident was related to give force to an exhortation to live a consistent Christian life. Another chief—a very fine-looking old man—told us that when he became a Christian his friends forsook him, and warned him that he would never be able to do without his numerous wives. But he was able to thank God for the gift of kind friends. He was often tempted to abstain from private devotions, but God had given him strength to overcome the tempter.

Open-air services were conducted in different parts of the village by two companies of friends, and at seven o'clock the united service was held in the chapel.

Our first halting-place on Monday was at Darman, where I was requested to settle a dispute between two Ashantis and a native. It appeared that one of the strangers had the misfortune to be the son of a woman who had contracted a debt with the native. The latter watched his opportunity and seized the unsuspecting traveller and baggage, as well as the baggage of a fellow-traveller. After hearing somewhat lengthy and tedious details of the transaction, I decided that it would be an act of gross injustice to retain the goods of the friend, and that as the package of Manchester goods belonging to the unfortunate son might be retailed at a price which would almost cover the amount of the debt, the creditor should take ten shillings from me and cry "quits." (As I write I marvel at my generosity, and am persuaded that I could not repeat such an act of folly!) The creditor demurred—probably he thought I might be induced to increase the amount. I got into my hammock, creditor repented, but had to wait till my return journey before receiving the cash.

We journeyed to Mansu, and stayed for the night at Government House, the key of which was kept by the king, who expressed his regret that the place was so comfortless. He himself would gladly entertain me. I decided otherwise, thanking him for his kind thought. After having taken some refreshment and making myself snug for the night, I was waited upon by his majesty and principal officers of state to hear a "palaver." His majesty, on behalf of a subject, *versus* a slave. I promptly gave the king to understand that my work was to try to teach subjects to respect their kings and chiefs, and to teach kings to rule well; I did not desire to undertake the work of a judge. His majesty quite understood, but as he expressed a very earnest desire that I would hear the case and merely pass an opinion, I consented. The case was as follows :—Some years previously one of his chiefs, who "was going to dead," desired to bequeath his money and trinkets to his nephew.[1] Well knowing that his life was rapidly drawing to a close, he sent for the king and said : "I wish my nephew to receive my property. But until he gets 'good sense' my head slave must hold the money and always be his friend." The chief died. Eight years passed away, but when the young man arrived at years of discretion, or had got "good sense," the money was not forthcoming to the full amount. The old slave declared that he had handed in all that he had received. I heard witnesses for the prosecution and then asked the slave what he had to say. He repeated his former statement, which his son would confirm. The son was called—the old man desired a few words privately beforehand. Judge decided otherwise. When questioned the son knew "nothing about this

---

[1] In this mysterious country the blood relationship between father and son is not always beyond dispute, hence property is handed to the son of a sister.

matter." The old man had one more witness who was many miles away. Judgment was pronounced against the old scamp, and the case referred to the District Commissioner, who subsequently issued a writ against him. His majesty thanked me for my words, and suggested that the slave was worthy of banishment. I had only to utter the word and the miserable wretch would have had to go. But, as he had committed no political offence and as I was not a judge, I could do nothing of the kind.

The following afternoon we reached Fesu. The population is composed of two distinct tribes—the Assins, natives of the district, and Adansi refugees, who had fled for protection from the Ashantis. The difference in the mode of house-building marked the two tribes; but both were agreed in their object of worship, both were deeply degraded and superstitious. In a spare hour I walked through the village and visited a fetish house; the priest was excessively nervous, and implored me not to enter. I did not stay to inquire into the reason of his fear. He may have thought that harm would come to his fetishes, or he may have thought that I would suffer. At any rate, I respected his wish and turned aside.

My visit to the town was quite unexpected. The junior minister of the circuit, the Rev. J. A. Markin, expressed his regret that he had not been informed of my purpose, for he had had the Christians from other villages the previous Sunday, and he would have been glad to have arranged for them to stay and hear the white man speak. I suggested that they might be summoned to return. Two boys were found who were willing to take a message to a village, twelve miles distant, for the sum of eighteenpence. Mr. Martin was grieved to hear of the extortionate demand; but I concluded that ninepence apiece for walking twenty-four miles was not extravagant payment, and so sanctioned the expenditure. The message sent was a verbal one, for none of the recipients would have been able to read a written communication. It was necessary to send a token that the messengers were *bona fide* messengers from the Osofu.[1] The insignia in this instance was an ebony ruler. By seven o'clock the next morning the lads had returned accompanied by the Christians. It was to be a field-day for them. The two thousand pagans with their dissolute king allowed the four native Christians to enjoy the greatest freedom, for the white man was with them. The little bamboo chapel was a perfect marvel of neatness; an exact model of it is before me as I write. I do not remember the exact size, but it was about fifteen feet by ten. The walls, doors, shutters, seats, and rafters were of bamboo, the roofing of palm branches. "What did it cost to erect this place?" I inquired of my economical assistant. After a slight pause, and with a half-inquiring, half-apologetic look on his

---

[1] Royal messengers are usually given an elephant's tail as a token of their royal mission.

face he replied, "Fourteen shillings and sixpence." And then, as if to account for this reckless expenditure, he explained that the reason he could not get it done for *nothing* was because his pagan labourers refused to work without payment.

I was anxious to ascertain what amount of influence Christianity exerted among the pagans. I felt then, as I feel now, that I could safely trust Mr. Markin to furnish me with an illustration. This is one. The chief of the place—whom it was my business to see, —a besotted specimen of humanity, had grievously offended a neighbouring chief, who naturally sought the earliest opportunity of "making palaver." The two met, accompanied by their leaders and followers, and spent much time in trying to settle the grievance, but their efforts were in vain. Finally they sent for the Osofu. He spent some hours in counsel with them; for if there is one thing an African likes more than another it is a good palaver. Eventually they agreed to accept the decision of Mr. Markin, and the "jury," viz., the headmen, required the offender to pay compensation amounting to £100. " Now," I asked, " why was it that you were asked to settle this matter ? Was it because you were the only educated man in the village, or was it because you are a Christian ? " " Undoubtedly because I am a Christian," was the answer. More than seven years have passed since this statement was made, and I have never had the slightest reason to question the value of it. Repeatedly, in various parts of the Colony,

I have unexpectedly come upon our people who have been engaged in adjusting differences of opinion in heathen families. The latter certainly know the native Christian, and although not themselves prepared to make the sacrifice which such a profession involves, they are willing to avail themselves of the services of the Christian in the hour of need.

Unlike the religions of other heathen countries, Fetishism is represented by very few idols. It is a most unusual thing to see a pagan adoring a block of wood or stone. No heathen temples adorn the land, no elaborate ritual accompanies the ceremonies, no sacred writings are found in which the traditional beliefs of the ancients might be expressed. The religion, which is one of the lowest forms in existence, consists mainly of superstitious beliefs—largely aided by witchcraft—which have been handed down from generation to generation by a succession of priests, who delude the credulous minds of the people by their fraudulent practices. Fetishism is essentially spirit worship, but of so debasing and demoralising a type as to be hardly distinguishable from devil worship. As stated in an earlier chapter, the heathen certainly acknowledge their belief in a Supreme Being, the Creator of all things, with Whom, however, it is quite impossible to hold any communication. They live in constant dread of subordinate deities, who are always prepared to visit with wrath the individual or nation at large.

The residences of these beings are known as Fetish. At the village of Aburi, twenty-four miles from the seat of government, is a swamp devoted to the fetish for the reason that snakes, credited with the possession of evil spirits, take up their residence there. Frequently the favourite residence of the spirits is a tree, which is carefully protected by a hedge, at the base of which may be seen large stones and pots of native workmanship containing the offerings of the devotees.

These fetishes are regarded as peculiarly sacred, and no true believer would dream of injuring them, lest some great calamity should befall him. On one occasion a huge reptile—measuring fourteen feet—entered the compound of a peasant who lived about a mile from our home. The man was naturally in great terror, and made all possible haste to the village to procure help. Among those who went to his assistance was a sportsman, armed with a gun. "What are you thinking of doing with that gun?" asked a priest who happened to form part of the company. "Shoot the snake!" "Don't," replied the priest. "I forbid you!" "Why?" "Because this is one of the fetish snakes which has wandered from the swamp; if you kill it, the spirit will kill you!" "Oh, I don't believe that!" said the sportsman, and with that fired a fatal shot. Nothing more was heard of the affair until some weeks later, when the whole village was startled by the news that the sacrilegious sportsman was dead.

By what means he lost his life is not definitely known, but to this day the natives believe that it was due to the retribution of the spirit. Those who know the country and the skill of the natives in administering poisons will not charge us with want of charity when we suggest that the evil spirit found ready agents in the persons of the priests in accomplishing his designs.

The great object of fetish worship is to propitiate the spirits and to seek their goodwill and protection. This accounts for the fact that at the entrance of nearly every town and village we find fetish altars, where offerings are made to the spirits. Similar offerings may also be seen at the entrance of cemeteries, and also at the houses of private individuals, more particularly of kings and chiefs. At a small village near Aburi there are three such fetishes guarding the chief's household. Two consist of native pots raised some four feet above the ground: in these a medicinal herb and some water are observed. The third is simply a large number of rams' heads strung together.

If any great calamity occurs or there is an outbreak of disease, it is at once thought that the spirits are angry and are venting their wrath on the unhappy people. In the early part of 1896 the village of Aburi was visited by small-pox. In its early stages it was not serious, and the mildest measures would have sufficed for its arrest. The villagers, however, were greatly alarmed, and declared that it was the work of an evil spirit who must be at once expelled from their midst. The priests advised the fetish dance. Processions were accordingly organised: tom-toms were called into requisition, and Kweku, Kodwo and Kobina, with their sisters Adwua, Ekua and Amba, vied with one another in most unearthly yells and gesticulations, in order that the "bad spirit" might be frightened away. Strange to say the desired end was not attained, the spirit would not leave, the small-pox still raged. What was to be done? "Oh," replied the priests, "many of your sheep and rams have dark skins, send them away to your 'bush' farms, for they are detaining the spirit. The suggestion was at once carried out, but still the disease remained. The villagers were in despair. "Of course the spirit does not go," said the priests, "every time he makes the attempt your cocks begin to crow, and he is thus called back. Kill all your cocks and then he will depart." This last order was not very strictly carried out, for though some of the innocent feathered bipeds suffered martyrdom and others replenished the poultry yard of the European, some few were allowed to remain. In the course of a few days the disease itself died out.

Witchcraft enters largely into the fetish religion and is much resorted to by the priests. We here give representations of the stock-in-trade of a priest; the originals formerly belonged to one who has renounced heathenism and has embraced

Christianity. It is largely by these and similar agencies that the priests exercise their power over their people. Rich men and chiefs have been known to pay a good price for sets similar to those here described, in order that they might increase their power.

Fetish No. 1 is used as a restorative in cases of fainting fits. The priest (who, by the way, is invariably a doctor) stands over his patient, smites him on the forehead with the instrument, and at the same time calls him by name. The apparently dying man is speedily brought back to health and strength.

No. 2 is said to be efficacious when a man wishes to protect his life in time of warfare. For example, there is a riot in a neighbouring town; shots are being fired on both sides, so much so that the ordinary passer-by stands a fair chance of being wounded. Business of urgent importance calls a man through the scene of carnage. He will naturally be running a very great risk; a shot, accidental or otherwise, may at least disfigure him. What is he to do? Happy thought, the priest has the very thing! With this charm our hero may boldly pass through the town, and by waving the bunch of rough flax above his head he will be able to scatter the shot in all directions save on his own person.

No. 3 is another charm used for the protection of life. The possessor is going on a journey; his enemy hears of it, and thinks it a good opportunity

GOLD COAST FETISHES.

for obtaining his revenge. He will now be able to kill the hated rival. |He goes to the priest and obtains from him poisonous herbs, of immense strength ; these he prepares in a prescribed manner, and then sprinkles across the path along which he knows his adversary must pass ; the moment the unsuspecting traveller places his feet upon the herbs he will certainly die. The foul designer, however, has not counted on the wonderful remedy here represented, therefore his labour is in vain ; and to his disgust his hated rival, by simply holding with both hands the fibrous charm, is marvellously protected and spared.

No 4. represents a restorative. A patient is seized with pains which suggest to our minds an attack of rheumatism. The fetish doctor is summoned ; his remedy is a perfect marvel of simplicity. Taking the two sticks he places them on the spot where the pain is felt and binds them firmly against the skin with the string. He then orders the patient to his couch, with the comforting assurance that in two or three days he "will be as well as ever he was."

No. 5 was taken from the wrist of a woman in the neighbourhood of Pram Pram (Accra). Having failed to restore the old lady to health and strength it was abandoned with disgust. Stern measures were also resorted to in the case of the fetish marked 6. My colleague, the Reverend S. C. Hall, observed it lying helplessly by the roadside at Fesu, Assin, and he wondered thereat. On inquiry he was informed that it was unmercifully beaten (its leg being broken in the chastisement) and unceremoniously turned out of house and home for having failed in its mission of arresting from the jaws of death a resident in that village. The price paid to the priest for the fetish and its two companions was £3.

The figure marked No. 7 was attached to the house which was placed at my disposal while staying at Bekwai Ashanti, in the early part of 1896. It was, I presume, intended to preserve the proprietor from all harm. No explanation can be given respecting the object marked 8. The upper part is evidently made to resemble the top of a human skull, the wires form the handles of eighty-eight pairs of rather neat little tongs, the jaws of which are covered by skin. The curiosity came from Ashanti during the expedition.

Figure No. 9 represents an instrument of death. Two men have a hot dispute over a trifling matter. The quarrel becomes so fierce that one of them, transported with rage, vows that his opponent must die. He procures this root with its miraculous properties from the priest, and forcing it into the ground repeats the name of the doomed man, whose decease is only a question of a few days. No. 10 is used for a similar purpose. But in this case the priest himself performs the awful deed. Taking the two sticks in his left hand, he slowly winds the string, and repeats the victim's name three or four times. Then putting the bundle on the ground, he places a stone upon it and gravely assures his dupe that the opponent's hours are numbered. In No. 11 we have a fetish which is also used for taking human life, but from less vindictive motives than in the instances just described. A relative is very ill, possibly has been ill for years. He has consulted all the doctors available, he has spent all his money in paying their fees, now there appears to be no hope of his recovery, and withal he has become a burden to his family. His relatives do not care for the expense and bother this illness involves; doctors' bills are decidedly objectionable. Accordingly the friends meet to take counsel; they speak of the illness, the incurable nature of the disease, the certainty that it will end in death, and at last they decide that as it is sure to terminate fatally, it would be as well if the patient died at once as at a later date. It is therefore unanimously agreed that he be put to death. How is it to be done? None of the members wish to deliberately accelerate the decease by violent measures, the fatal act must be such that every member may take part in it. The head of the family, in the sight and with the consent of the rest, takes the fetish, and holding the two pieces of iron as far apart as possible, he repeats the man's name several times, and then thrusts them into the earth. Whereupon their burdensome relative naturally "shuffles off this mortal coil."

Figure No. 12 represents a fetish which is chiefly

used as an oracle. A traveller, wishing to journey to Ashanti, is anxious to know whether his plans will succeed. How is it possible to ascertain? We shall see. Taking a fowl he kills it and pours the warm blood over the bowl; then, having thoroughly cleansed himself, he enters his private chamber, and having closed the door, stands in the centre of the room with the fetish on his head and addresses the spirit thus: "Shall I go to Ashanti or not? If I go, shall I live or die? Shall I prosper in my undertaking?" and so on. The spirit working through the fetish relieves the inquirer from all anxiety concerning his movements.

Figure No. 13 represents a hunter's fetish. Before setting out on an expedition, the hunter takes this vessel and pours palm-oil over it and places it in the sunlight. In a short time he watches it intently, and there, on the surface of the vessel, he sees the skin of the animal which he will shoot during the day. He has but to take his gun and journey to the bush, where he will find the accommodating animal actually waiting for him. This remarkable fetish never fails. A colleague once met a hunter returning empty-handed after long absence, notwithstanding the customary consultation. "Where is your game?" asked my friend. "Oh," replied the man of sport, "my mouth no want meat, so I no shoot him!"

Figure No. 14 suggests one of the many devices resorted to in various parts of Akwapim, in cases

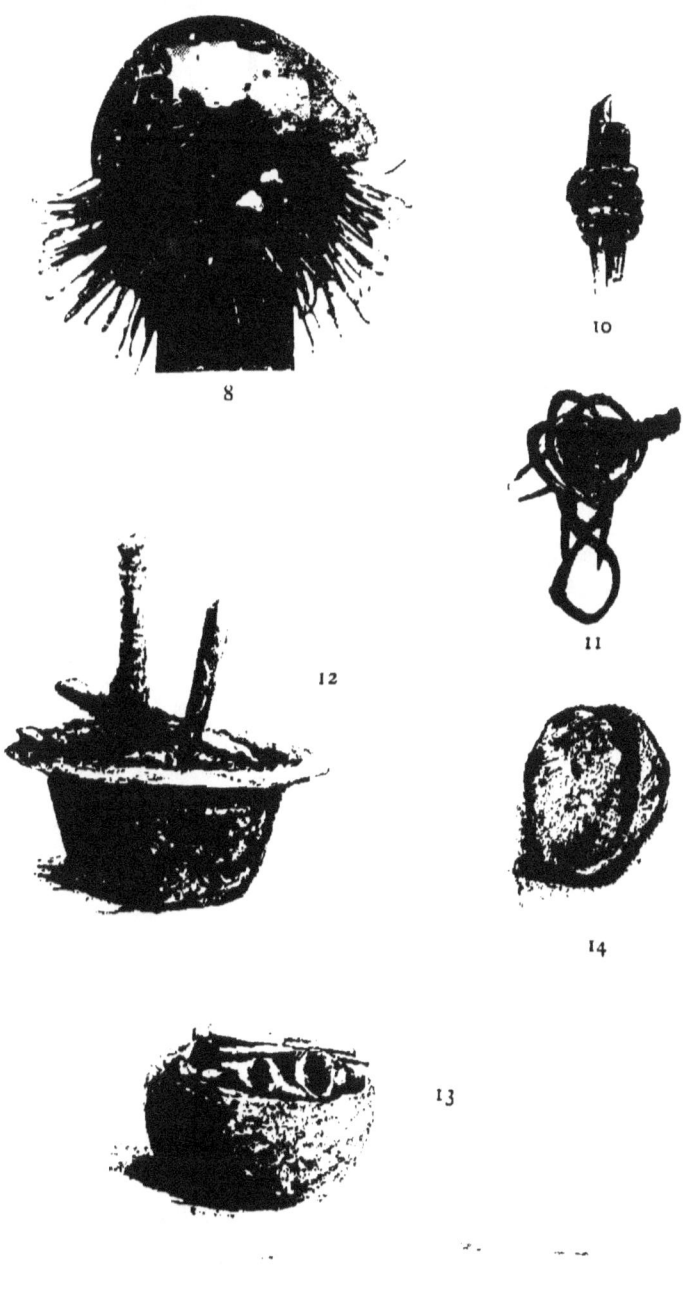

GOLD COAST FETISHES.

[*To face page* 128.

of native trials. A man has been poisoned wilfully. There is, however, no evidence by which to trace the guilty party, but it is suspected that some one residing in the immediate neighbourhood has perpetrated the crime. The course adopted for bringing the murderer to justice is as follows :—Branches of palm trees are woven into the shape of a basket and the fetish is placed therein. The whole town is then summoned, and the basket, with its contents, is placed on the head of a young maiden who is made to stand in the centre of the company. In an incredibly short space of time the medium of the spirit will walk straight up to one of the bystanders and proclaim him guilty. It will be useless for the accused to protest his innocence, for the proof will be regarded as indisputable. There are other expedients which are sometimes resorted to in native trials. For example, one man charges another before a chief with a crime, but the evidence adduced is not sufficient to establish the charge. He is required to take an oath as to the truth of his statements. Now, if the accused in his turn takes an oath that he is innocent, he is required to prove his innocence by means of an ordeal. He must do one of two things, either he must drink a decoction obtained from odum wood, or chew a piece of the wood itself, and drink a bowl of water immediately afterwards. Odum is said to contain a substance which may poison, or at least act as an emetic. If the person subjected to the ordeal merely vomits, he is innocent, if, on the contrary, he is attacked with violent pains in the stomach, he is proved guilty. Just before the Ashanti war of 1873, the chiefs of Ashanti-Akim sent to their brethren in Akim, warning them to be on their guard, as war was about to be declared against them. The king heard of it and charged them with the offence; they denied it. He therefore subjected them to the odum test, with the result that six of them were found guilty and put to death.

In the early part of 1896 a stranger visited Aburi. He professed to be a fetish priest of extraordinary influence. He declared that through his agency thieves and other criminals were always discovered, that no one was ever known to escape. It so happened that there had been a theft in the village; accordingly some of the villagers requested him to discover the thief. He readily consented. A large company assembled; it was believed that the thief was among them. The stranger stood before them and produced from a small bag sundry herbs and pieces of wood. From these he prepared a poisonous drug; then, taking a small calabash (one produced by himself for the special purpose) he said: "I am about to pour a few drops of this poison in the bowl and fill up with water and drink it. If no harm comes to me you may rest assured that I am innocent. If, on the other hand, I am poisoned, do not pity me, for the guilty deserves punishment. If I survive I shall repeat the dose, fill up with water and pass it round to each of you, and you must all partake in turn. The man who suffers from the poison is undoubtedly guilty." The magician, however, wisely omitted to inform the wonder-stricken throng that his juggler's gourd was bored with a small hole, through which the poison was, on occasions, allowed to disappear. No one observed the safety valve; no one suspected it. As soon as the poison disappeared, he discreetly placed a finger over the hole, poured in the water and drained off the contents. His innocence of the theft enabled him to survive, and the test was similarly applied to a score of men standing near. Eventually he came to one whom he imagined to be the culprit; the safety-valve was now closed, the unfortunate man received the contents, violent pains ensued, and he was proclaimed the thief.

Travellers at the Gold Coast frequently meet with spiritual agents in human form. The bodies of the media are covered with white powder; it is difficult to realise how hideous they can make themselves. Arms, face, chest, back and legs are of a grayish-white colour; the natural colour of the skin is exposed round the eyes and mouth, and the effect is indescribable. In the midst of an admiring crowd, they dance, gesticulate wildly and behave generally like demoniacs. It is a most sad sight; both men and women become subjects of this spell, and sometimes in their frenzy they go to the length of attempting to divest themselves of all their clothing (which at best is very scanty) unless a spectator with the faintest regard for decency intervenes.

At stated times festivals are held in honour of the spirits. They are popularly known as "customs." Some of them are of a very dangerous character, and often lead to personal injury. Imagine a band of maniacs in a drunken state rushing recklessly to and fro, and at the same time throwing large knives up into the air. Small wonder that in their bungling they fail to catch them, and that accidents occur.

These customs are accompanied by dancing, drunkenness, and notorious immorality. Quite recently the natives of a village near us invited their neighbours to a heathen dance. The invitation was accepted. Three men presided over the tom-toms and furnished the instrumental music, while others, led by a skilled performer, moved in curved lines. The customary crowd of admirers applauded. Occasionally one of the gentler sex would step out from among the onlookers and mark an arm of one of the dancers with powdered cam-wood, after which they embraced. This mark of distinction signified that the woman was willing to prostitute herself during the three days the guests would remain in the village.

The most important festival of the whole year is known as the Yam Custom, which is held in September when the new yams are fully grown. The heathen, headed by the priests, march in solemn procession to the fetish altars to present their first-fruits as offerings to the gods; then returning to their village they spend their time in "rioting and drunkenness" in "chambering and wantonness." Not until the close of the custom are any allowed to partake of the new yams.

In Ashanti, before its conquest, the natives abstained from food on the first and fifth days of the custom, but drank excessively. On these occasions a criminal was slain in order that he might go as a messenger to the deceased kings. Then also the king ate of the new yams. On stated days, the natives sprinkled themselves with water, and processions were formed in honour of the protecting spirits. During the festival human victims were taken to the plantations and there sacrificed in order that some of the blood might flow into the holes from whence the yams were taken. On the last day the king's wives paraded the streets of Kumasi, and the subjects were allowed to partake of their new crops.

CHAPTER IX

THE FIRST SERIOUS BREAK IN THE EUROPEAN STAFF—A JOURNEY TO THE GOLD MINES—EXTRACTS FROM REPORTS—PEACE-MAKING BETWEEN CONVERTS—ADVANTAGES OF AFRICAN WORKERS AMONG AFRICANS—THE ARRIVAL OF THE REVEREND A. W. HALL—INDUSTRIAL TRAINING—COMMERCIAL INTERESTS IN WEST AFRICA NOT ESSENTIALLY SELFISH

IN the early part of November the district suffered an inestimable loss in the removal of the Reverend S. C. Hall, who, after a series of protracted attacks of fever, was ordered home. Our friend was most reluctant to leave, but the doctor's orders were peremptory. I believe that even to-day Mr. Hall suffers from his residence at the Gold Coast; he certainly has had repeated attacks of malarial fever since his return home.

I confess to many a pang of regret as I journeyed to Anamabu to pack his removable effects, and to dispose of the remainder. To what extent the Colony suffers in the removal of experienced men in the various services few can imagine. In a part of the Mission field which is subject to so much change it is difficult to effect permanent benefits, but Mr. Hall succeeded, as subsequent experience abundantly testified. Our beautiful church at Anamabu would probably not have been in existence to-day, but that the superintendent's direction was attracted to the odd manner in which the roof had been constructed, and which threatened to collapse and force the walls from their perpendicular position. This work, in which he was ably assisted by his native colleague, and the consequent exposure to the sun, cost Mr. Hall his health, and the district an invaluable Missionary. But the permanent benefits were to be seen in the improved organisation of the circuit which at that time embraced no fewer than thirty-one churches and upwards of a hundred centres where the Gospel was proclaimed, to say nothing of the improved state of the day and Sunday Schools. The native colleagues were trained in methods of account keeping, and to-day are enabled to present returns which are models of neatness and order.

In December a journey to the Missions at the Gold Mines was considered advisable. Reference has already been made to the work begun by Dr. Martin of the Gie Appantoo Mining Company. Mention should also be made of the fact that the directors, with Mr. Samuel Causton at their head, took the greatest possible interest in the evangelistic work. They felt that they could not be so absorbed in their own temporal interests as to have no regard for the spiritual interests of their employés and the natives of the Wassaw region.

As I have already dealt at considerable length with the object of my missionary tours I shall omit any reference to the reasons that led to this particular journey, and venture a few observations on the gold-mining industry. I must, however, add that I felt the utmost sympathy for my fellow countrymen, so far removed from the comparative civilisation of the sea-board, especially as I could not but reflect that the work at a distance of 120 feet below the surface of the earth must be particularly trying to their health and constitutions.

We have seen that prior to the discovery of gold-fields in other parts of the world the European nations with the forced labour of slaves, were enabled to obtain from West Africa enormous quantities of gold. We have suggested that our supply is even now well-nigh inexhaustible. No one asks why we are not successful in obtaining the precious metal in paying quantities, for it is well known that the climate proves an almost insuperable barrier.

Will the output ever prove remunerative? Most certainly! How? By the employment of skilled native labour. The most remunerative mine at the present time is that which is managed by a native. There are no interruptions in the management, for the manager is never invalided home. And it is just possible that a native can get more work out of native employés than can a European. At the present time there are young men, natives of the

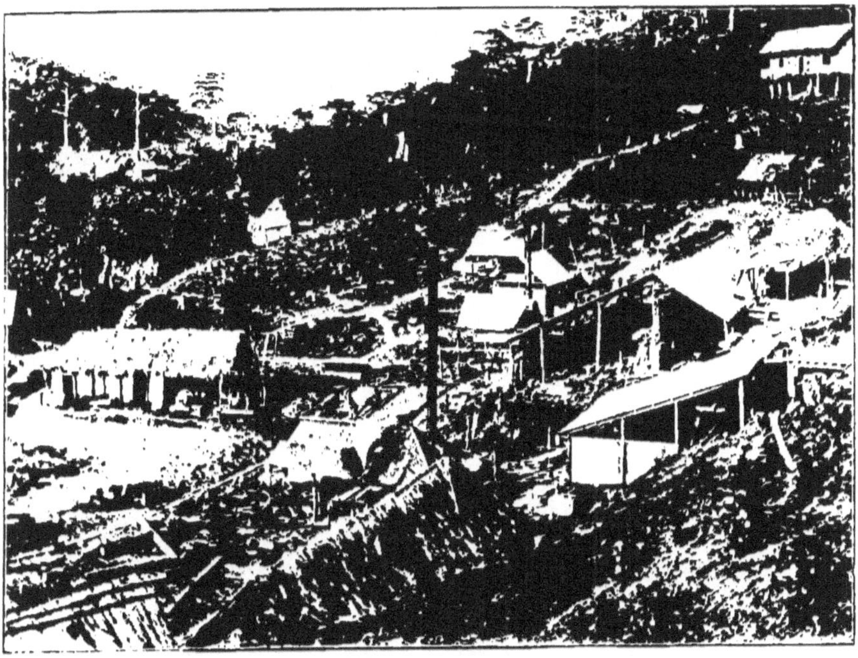

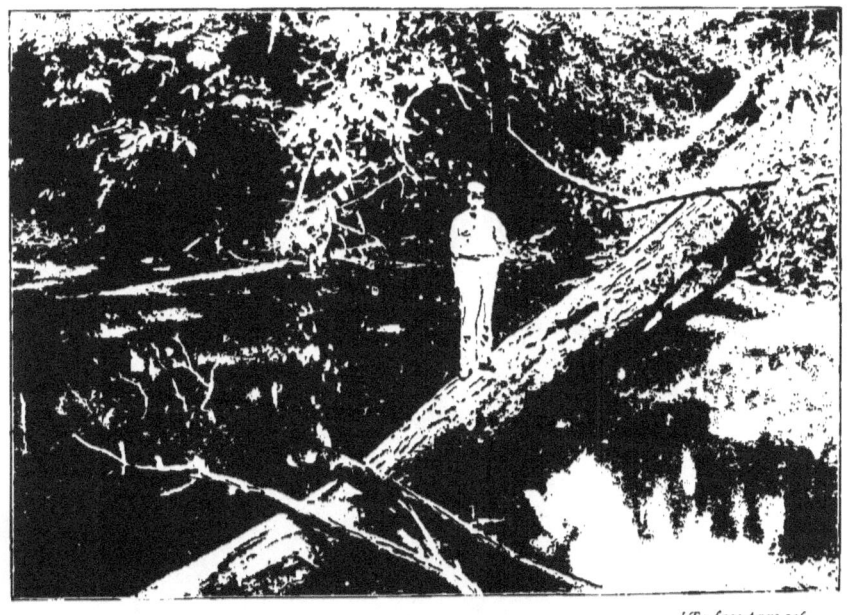

Essaman Gold Mines.

[To face page 136.

Tree Bridge, River Whin, Gold Coast Colony.

Gold Coast, who are turning their attention to mining engineering in England; in another generation the number will be much greater, and probably by that time native companies will be formed to supply the necessary machinery, and then gold-mining will pay.

But I am anxious,—almost as anxious as if I had shares in a Gold Coast Company—that the work should prove remunerative now. And my anxiety arises not merely for the sake of companies that have ventured so much upon their undertakings, but also for the future of the Colony itself. How is this to be accomplished?

I would, in the first place, suggest that the greatest possible attention be given to the health of the European employés. This, of course, is the case already; no English company would fail to give due consideration to the health and comfort of its representatives. But it has sometimes occurred to us that the residences in the neighbourhood of the mines might be constructed with greater regard to hygienic principles. For instance, the living rooms, and particularly the bedrooms, might, with advantage, be arranged at a height of not less than nine feet from the ground. For though pestilence at all times "walks in darkness, and destruction wastes at noon-day," the malaria is supposed to be much more dense, as it creeps along the surface of the earth. The enclosures in which the houses are erected, and which should be as extensive as practicable, should be kept free from weeds and decayed vegetation, and arrangements made whereby a supply of vegetables and fruit is ensured. Generous diet has already been advised, extravagance is greatly to be deprecated. The house should be furnished so as to give it a home-like appearance. We usually study comfort in this land, why should we not in a country where we are sometimes tempted under the influence of malarial fevers to imagine that life is not worth living? The "staff" should be sufficiently strong to be prepared for one member to take an occasional rest from ordinary duties, and, with a company of Englishmen so dependent upon medical aid, the doctor should have a comrade-in-arms.

Notwithstanding the greatest possible precautions that are taken to preserve health, it is too much to expect that the staff will continue to work uninterruptedly. The ideal Coast subject, be he "tall and spare," "short and thick-set," "dark" or "fair" will, perhaps at a moment when he is most needed, be at least temporarily disabled. In some cases his return to the mines is strictly forbidden. How exceedingly awkward for the company concerned if the officer in question proves to be the manager! And how increasingly awkward if, as sometimes happens, the vacancy is filled by a gentleman who adopts new methods in the management of the mines, and finds it necessary to considerably modify the methods of his predecessor! Such a modification may involve the importation of costly machinery, which may find its way to the bottom of the river Ancobra, and then what vexation of spirit, what waste of time and money! and the unfortunate Colony is once more placed under a ban.

To provide against the possibility of disappointments, the results of a change in policy, it might be worth while to engage permanently the services of a consulting engineer, familiar with the mining centres, to whom recommendations for such changes might be referred.

It requires no small amount of nerve for a Missionary to write upon such a subject as the gold mining industry, especially as it is quite natural to imagine that the Coast-miner may smile at the suggestions herein offered. But I have had repeated conversations with gentlemen who will never visit the Coast, but who have nevertheless ventured considerable sums of money, and have sometimes had good reason to lose heart. I have been asked to offer suggestions with a view to the preservation of health, and other hints that may be of practical service to those who take a practical interest in a country which has "wealth above and below ground."

The following paragraphs are culled from the Report for the year 1890:—

"The Report . . . . . presents many features of interest, and one or two of sadness. . . . . While we rejoice in a larger income we are distressed by the many calls for help. These come from all parts, coast and interior; and to many we can only send back the sorrowful reply—'We would gladly help, but are unable.' Already our Mission limits are almost conterminous with those of the Colony, on the seaboard, while up country we are in places beyond them. But we are anxious to go forward in answer to the appeals from the interior. Our forces are small. Over this wide area we have had only three resident Europeans and fifteen native ministers. Now, to our sorrow, two of the latter have left our ranks, while one (the Rev. T. B. Freeman), who had toiled for many years in his adopted country, has entered into his reward.

"Cape Coast is our oldest circuit. Wesley, the chief chapel, has been crowded, notwithstanding the fact that another Mission has begun services at hand There is an earnest missionary spirit among the people, and they intend doing more aggressive work. The missionary subscriptions have largely increased."

The Elmina, Aburah, and Anamabu circuits furnished illustrations of the power of Christianity over Fetishism. Several conversions of notable priests were reported.

"Accra is by far the largest town on the coast, and the seat of government. Our congregations have become so large at Wesley that it is necessary to build a gallery to accommodate the worshippers who at present are unable to gain admission."

Under Day Schools " We report an increase all along the line, both in numbers and in efficiency. Three of the central schools are entirely self-supporting. Calls are being made for higher training, and, as far as possible, we are endeavouring to meet them. We are intensely anxious to provide agricultural and industrial training for our boys. By this means we hope to raise up a more industrious and sturdy race. But we need considerable help from England to do this work thoroughly. We are confident that any outlay under this head would prove most profitable.

"We are greatly troubled at the condition of female education: we have not a solitary girls' school of any size. This work can be done thoroughly by English women alone. Could we but secure the sympathy and help of some English ladies here there would be a revolution in the female world in a few years, and that revolution is sorely needed.

" Cape Coast holds the proud position of premier school in the Colony for the third successive year. It has recently passed an examination by H.M. Inspector at 99·3 per cent. The girls' department has altogether collapsed, owing to the resignation of the mistress in charge. The junior teachers of the school have rendered valuable service to schools at Dunkwa, Chama, and Dix Cove. At Elmina we suffer greatly owing to the free educational system of the Roman Catholic Mission. The Accra school has been entirely reorganised. Seven new teachers have been added to the staff. Several new subjects have been added to the syllabus, and we hope to make it a good substantial school.

"The Volta Mission was started in the latter part of the year. Earnest requests were sent by the members of a small independent church in Kpong that we would receive them. In October they formally came to us, and their building was transferred to the District Synod. We number forty-one members and fifteen on trial, with seventy-two catechumens. We have also started work at Adda, at the mouth of the Volta. This town of 7,000 inhabitants is in dense heathenism. Buildings have been secured, and will shortly be opened. In this Mission we have a basis for fine aggressive work in the interior. Already several requests from heathen centres have been sent in, but at present our lack of funds compels us to turn a deaf ear to them.

"Vernacular literature has progressed but slowly, as the translators have been so fully occupied with their pastoral work. A Fanti reading book has been prepared and the second catechism has been translated and both are now being printed. We hope that the New Testament will be completed in the course of the year. A Gâ (Accra) hymn book is also being prepared. We could wish for more enthusiasm on the part of some of our native friends."

Here let us record the account of a "palaver"

IX A DISPUTE BETWEEN EUODIAS AND SYNTYCHE 143

between two Christians which is not given in the Annual Report, but is furnished by the superintendent who assisted in the settlement of the matter. Vendors in the market-place are for the most part representatives of the gentler sex. It sometimes happens that two or more will engage in a hot dispute. Their angry voices may be heard above the din of a thousand of their sex peaceably engaged in lawful trade. There was an occasion when, as at Philippi, sisters Euodias and Syntyche were not "of the same mind." "Softly, softly," said the one to the other, "we are Christians; let us go to the minister." To the minister they went. The elders of the church were summoned. And then for a time superfluous steam was allowed to escape in yells, shrieks, and frantic gesticulations; care was taken that the disputants were separated by at least a table or a desk, so as to prevent the one from doing bodily harm to the other. In a few moments comparative order was restored, the whole case was stated, the opinion of the elders expressed, and the outside world knew nothing of what had occurred. My friend, who relates the incident, suggests that the altercation might prove a shock to refinement, but the termination was infinitely more satisfactory than are the petty feuds between families which are sometimes allowed to smoulder in this highly-favoured land.

Reference is made in the foregoing extracts to the crowded congregations at two of our centres. Our church, while recognising the importance of other agencies on the Mission field, endeavours to give due prominence to the great command of Christ to proclaim His truth to the heathen. In this work we have to depend more upon native than upon European agency. The work of the European Missionary is to prepare native workers, as will be seen by the following extract from the handbook of instructions to Missionaries :—" The General Letter of November 3rd, 1877, gives directions that the European ministers be relieved as much as possible of the exhaustive duties of pastors to the native churches. Their function is rather to train up from among the converts men who shall be fitted for the trying and intricate work of native pastors. It will be practicable with an increasing native ministry to leave the European Missionary free for general supervision and direction." Hence a safe rule to be observed is never to do anything one's self which a native can do. The European Missionary is the drill sergeant, reducing the recruits to order; but never absent when his comrades are called to arms. Our native preachers are, as a rule, " workmen that need not to be ashamed." Some preach well in English, but in the vernacular they exert great power. The way they can grapple with the conscience, apply the truth, and help the seeker in search of Christ is most gratifying. Our motto has long been " The Fanti for the Fantis." While I am convinced that we shall not be able to dispense

IX IMPORTANCE OF DEVELOPING NATIVE MINISTRY 145

entirely with European supervision for a generation or more, I am equally convinced that we shall have to trust increasingly to native preachers. The European staff, which is, comparatively speaking, much more costly than is the native, is liable to interruptions at any time. The frequent absences on account of furlough seriously affect our work. In nine instances out of ten the European has scarcely been enabled to understand the manners and customs of the natives before he is removed, either to England, or to that country from whose "bourn no traveller returns." Hence the importance of developing a native ministry.

But there is a still greater reason than those already given. The life of the consistent native Christian is a greater testimony to the power of the Gospel than the life of the European ever can be. The life of the devoted white man is in danger of being misunderstood. By the native he is placed on a pedestal far above the poor black man. The native ascribes to superior nature and to propitious environment, that which ought to be ascribed to the transforming power of the Gospel of Christ. But the consistent life of the man of colour appeals to his fellow-countryman. He is skin of their skin; his life is known from his youth upward; he is trained under conditions known to them, and similar to theirs. In his case his associates can but attribute to the Gospel the changed life he lives. He is a standing advertisement to the Gospel he

L

preaches, and his message gains cogency from the fact of his life. When a man can get up and say, "You know me and my former life; you witness the life I now live. This life I live, not of myself, but through the power of the Christ whom I proclaim"—the effect is conviction. Preaching, as a missionary agency, we put in the foreground, and in honour we prefer our native brethren.

In the early part of 1891 our General Superintendent took his final leave of the district. By his most statesmanlike administration of the affairs of the Synod, no less than by his well-known brotherliness towards his colleagues, he completely won the confidence of the workers connected with our Mission, and it was with feelings of the deepest regret that we accompanied him to the steamer *Benin* for the last homeward voyage. Mr. Halligey has many friends in various parts of the Coast. His ministerial probation was spent at Free Town, Sierra Leone, in the early "seventies," and in 1885 he was entrusted with the charge of the Lagos District, and soon became familiar with the famous Yoruba country. Two years later the care of the Gold Coast District was added to his responsibilities; so that it is unnecessary to say that few men in any service have such an acquaintance with West Africa as has the Rev. J. T. F. Halligey, whose contributions to the Royal Geographical Society have been acknowledged by his admission as a Fellow. It is almost too much to hope, and far too much to expect, that he will return to his old sphere of labour; but should circumstances ever admit, no Missionary will be more universally welcomed, for no Missionary was more universally esteemed.

The vacancy created by Mr. Hall's permanent departure was filled by a namesake, Reverend Arthur W. Hall, of Didsbury College, Manchester. As I write, my study is—not tidy, and I think, with perfect envy, of the method and neatness of that Missionary brother. He certainly was the neatest, and, if I may be permitted to add, one of the most methodical Missionaries of my time. But method and neatness are not the only requisite qualifications in a Missionary, and Mr. Hall possessed others, as we shall see. His first appointment was to Salt Pond, a town growing considerably in importance, five miles to the east of Anamabu. It was hoped that he would have been enabled to remain at Salt Pond to assist in the development of the work there; but as the present writer was, a few months later, strongly advised by his medical attendant to take his furlough, Mr. Hall returned to Cape Coast to take charge of the schools and the exchequer.

Reference was made in the last chapter to the expressed need of the development of industrial training among our young people. It was felt that there was much truth in the reproach that education, as given in our schools, had a tendency to unfit our lads for useful occupations in handicrafts. We have been told that our schools simply glutted the markets with clerks. For our own part, we have most earnestly wished that there was even a shadow of truth in this statement. Were this really the case, we, as a Mission, should not find so much difficulty, when desiring teachers and catechists for our own work, in competing with merchants in their tempting salaries to our young men. And further, we should not have expressed the strong feeling of disgust that the merchants and the Government alike so constantly employed young men without references from us. But this, nevertheless, has been our experience, so great was their desire to employ the candidates, with or without testimonials. The fact of the matter was, we could not supply the vacancies in offices throughout the district. But apart from this consideration, we could not shut our eyes to the fact that the overwhelming majority of the artisan class were illiterate; it was equally evident that our educated youths did not follow the useful employments as we wished. The remedy was to be found in combining technical with elementary education.

Mention must here be made of the invaluable work of the Basle Missionary Society at Christiansborg. The artisans trained in their workshops are found at Accra and at the Niger Delta, and in other parts of the Coast. We could wish that our own Mission had such a history in this department.

A very humble beginning in this direction had,

indeed, been made at Cape Coast during the previous year. The building of the new school and the supply of the necessary furniture had furnished employment for a carpenter. A very capable workman was found in a native of the town, and an arrangement was made for a few of the senior lads to spend two half days a week in the workshop. It fell to Mr. Hall's lot to develop this important branch of our work. The care of the Sunday Schools had by this time been handed over to the native ministers, so that the new Missionary was enabled to devote greater attention to the day schools.

It was evident from the very first that Mr. Hall meant business. I had scarcely reached England when a letter followed, stating that the sum of £50 would be required to give the new work a good beginning. The amount was very promptly made up by Mr. A. L. Jones, who is known as the Napoleon of West African commerce, the late Mr. John Edgar, of the Royal Niger Company, and Mr. Alexander Miller, of the Niger Company and the Gold Coast. The result at Cape Coast was most gratifying.

I should like to relate the circumstance under which I met the late Mr. Edgar. It was at a missionary meeting at which he took the chair. In the course of his address the chairman pointed out the various ways in which the peoples of West Africa ministered to the needs of England in sending home the produce of the country. He concluded by saying that a country which ministered so much to our temporal necessities should have great claims upon our Christian sympathy. I am ashamed to say that up to that moment I scarcely knew the name of the chairman, and I certainly had not had the remotest idea that he was commercially connected with Africa. But I ventured in my address to say that I stood in need of £15 to enable me to carry out a pet scheme. The amount was readily promised by Mr. Edgar, and was repeated yearly until his decease.

The incident may appear trifling in itself but it is mentioned for the reason that I wish to record a most emphatic protest against those who teach the doctrine that commercial relations with Africa are purely selfish. I have repeatedly had occasion —in a very modest way, certainly—to feel the pulse of those who have business connections with West Africa, but I do not remember meeting with a merchant who was altogether regardless of the welfare of the natives. I have met with many who have taken the deepest interest in their advancement.

My good friend Mr. Jones, whose most generous sympathy with all good work in West Africa is well known, most modestly assures me that his assistance has been given from a purely business point of view. It is only natural that I should say that financial assistance of this kind is an excellent

CASTLE OF ST GEORGE, ELMINA. [Page 92.

YOUNG CARPENTER'S WORK. INDUSTRIAL EDUCATION. [To face page 150.

investment. Apart from philanthropic considerations, the uplifting of the people of Africa more than repays the benefactors, but I am inclined to think that Mr. Jones not only undertook his own, but the responsibilities of others by his generosity.

The new enterprise received a temporary check towards the end of the year. Mr. Hall was prostrated by a second attack of fever; and but for the timely visit of our friend Price, who called on his return voyage from England, it is more than possible that the terrible climate would have claimed another victim. The invalid was ignorant of the seriousness of the attack, and for three days he was "in the balance." The prompt and constant attention of Dr. Prout, and the careful nursing by a sympathetic colleague, undoubtedly snatched Mr. Hall from the brink of death. The invalid was ordered home, no one dreaming that he would think of returning, least of all the medical attendant who subsequently informed us that he considered it would have been quite unnecessary to recommend the Missionary to seek another sphere of labour. Three months' rest in England, however, proved sufficient to restore health and strength, and we had the satisfaction of welcoming our colleague back early the following year.

CHAPTER X

THE MISSIONARY IS JOINED BY HIS WIFE—THE URGENT NEED OF LADY WORKERS IN AFRICA—SUGGESTIONS RESPECTING THE SANITATION OF THE COLONY—A JOURNEY TO THE ABURI SANATORIUM, AND AN ACCOUNT OF THE CROBOE HEATHEN CUSTOMS

In the meantime I had taken to myself—" for better" certainly!—a wife. I must honestly confess that I was quite prepared to follow the example of other West African Missionaries, when taking that important step, and to say to the Gold Coast: " I have married a wife, and therefore cannot come ; I pray thee have me excused." I am, however, extremely thankful that Mrs. Kemp decided to take part in the important work.

The wisdom of taking European ladies to the West Coast is sometimes questioned. A Government officer once said to me, " The only ladies who ought to be permitted to go to West Africa are disagreeable mothers-in-law!" I felt almost tempted to reply : "Among all my European acquaintances in the Colony I know no one who more distinctly requires the surveillance of a mother-in-law than yourself!" Seriously, there are two sides to this question. Given a moderate amount of employment, a woman does not suffer more than does a man; this is largely due to the fact that the gentler sex are more prudent in a treacherous climate, and, from the nature of things, are less exposed to the sun and the rains; possibly, too, they have less of that anxiety which is the result of responsibility. Not that I would for one moment suggest that the wives do not enter most sympathisingly into their husbands' plans; they are probably more philosophic about the little worries in official life.

On the other hand, we have met with those to whom the separation from the husband for fourteen months would mean excessive cruelty. For the mental strain during the period of enforced absence would probably prove much more serious than would a corresponding term of residence at the Gold Coast. I may, however, be permitted to say that the motive which prompted my wife to undertake missionary work was not in order that she might be spared the separation; that would have been obviated by accepting a ministerial charge in England, for, apart from infirmities which might prevent the designation to a charge, no Wesleyan minister is ever without a church, as no Wesleyan church is ever without a minister. Nor was it undertaken because the Society required such service, for the Society requires no more from the wives of its missionaries than does the Government from the wives of its officers. No, the work was undertaken because of its supreme importance. I am afraid I have written egotistically; if I have, I regret it, but I wish to impress my readers with the fact that the most important work at the Gold Coast is (European) women's work among (native) women. I have sometimes amused my personal friends by saying that my sole reason for going to Africa as a married man was for the purpose of taking care of my wife who, as a Missionary, was to do by far the more important work of the two; the fact remains nevertheless.

The following paragraph is copied from the Minutes of evidence taken before the Select Committee on the West Coast of Africa, May 31st, 1842. *Chairman* (Viscount Sandon): " Can you state the nature of the difficulties which the Missionaries have experienced in promoting the improvement of the natives?"

Rev. Dr. Beecham: "I would observe, that the degradation of the female sex is one of the great obstacles with which the missionaries have to contend in their endeavours to improve the people; the women are treated as inferior beings, as mere creatures of convenience, and are grossly ignorant: many of the young men are now receiving education, but the females are not being improved and elevated in the same proportion. Three of the schools to which I have adverted are female schools, and the wives of the Missionaries have exerted themselves laudably, according to the opportunities they have had; but still one of the great desiderata for that part of the country, is the introduction of a more comprehensive and efficient system for the improvement and elevation of the female sex, from that state of deep degradation in which they are found."

We honour the memory of the Missionaries' wives of those early days. The results of their devotion are seen to-day, and had there been a succession of lady-workers up to the present time, our experience would not have been as deplorable as it has been. We regret to have to remark that the three schools above referred to disappeared. We had not a female teacher, native or European, devoted entirely to elementary education, and as a result the proportion of female to male scholars was only ten per cent. That this discreditable condition of affairs was due to our apparent lack of practical sympathy is abundantly attested by the fact that the result of one year's experiment changed the percentage from ten to twenty-five.

Mention must here be made of the invaluable service to the females by the Lutheran Missionaries and their wives. It has been said that the British territory at the Gold Coast is not really a Colony. Truer words were never written—nor sadder. We have not colonised, so much the worse for that country. "The only redeeming feature about the Coast is that it is a splendid place to leave!" says the Colonial officer. Who can blame him? But to the honour of the Basle Missionaries be it spoken they have, in many instances, made it practically the land of their adoption. They, with their wives and families, have exerted a mighty influence for good, and here again have been strong where we have been weak. It must be stated that the operations of the Basle Missionaries have been, for the most part, confined to the eastern, as our principal work has been done in the western, part of the Colony.

Reference must also be made to the love and devotion of the nuns of the Lyons Mission. No one can have known them without being struck with their noble spirit of self-sacrifice. Truly they "count not their lives dear unto them," and their work among the native girls and women is certainly beyond all praise.

I shall be forgiven if, as a Protestant, I say that I could not quite endorse all their theological teaching. And so we did not wonder that the saintly Sister Ignatius, to whom reference has already been made, should very frankly tell my wife, soon after her arrival at Cape Coast, that she was "extremely *sorry*" to see her. The Lady Superior was held in the highest esteem for her work's sake, and no one, outside her own religious circle, more truly regretted her death than did the residents at the Methodist Mission House.

But apart from theological differences there was one defect in their system, which from the very nature of things was altogether unavoidable. The nuns could not teach the native wives that they should be the helpmates of their husbands. They might indeed teach, as doubtless the priests, and as the writer had taught earlier, that St. Paul insisted that the husband should regard the wife as "his own flesh," and that he should therefore treat her with the consideration that is due to the "weaker vessel." But example is better than precept, and the lesson is far more effectively taught by the husband and wife conjointly than by the spinster or bachelor.

And so we venture to suggest that all who have the least faith in missionary enterprise, and can in the slightest degree realise the condition of the female sex in heathen lands, must recognise that this branch of our work is of the greatest importance.

The news which greeted us on our arrival at Cape Coast in January was anything but reassuring. The new General Superintendent of our Mission, the Reverend H. H. Richmond, who had been on the Coast only six weeks, was seized with an illness so serious as to render his immediate return to England imperative. Eighteen months of great physical suffering terminated in death. The loss to the Mission was very serious, for Mr. Richmond was a Missionary of great experience, and had travelled in West Africa in the early part of his ministerial life. But how insignificant was our loss compared with the loss to the widow and family!

The temporary charge of the Mission was entrusted to me. The duty was undertaken with great diffidence; but I was much encouraged and assisted by the sympathy and co-operation of the members of the Annual Synod; and at the conclusion of the sitting a memorial was forwarded to the Missionary Committee that I might be appointed to the permanent charge.

This gives me an opportunity of paying a tribute of esteem to the General Secretary of our Society, who had charge of the African Mission District, the Reverend Marshall Hartley. The official communications from his pen were characterised by their charm of unofficial brotherliness, and although paragraphs of a purely legislative character have been printed for the guidance of the European and native Missionaries in that district, yet the originals have been most religiously preserved for the sake of the expressions of sympathy and confidence which they contain. How greatly such letters are valued by the Missionary, so far removed from headquarters, none but the recipients can conceive. When the Representative of the Society has the entire confidence of the Committee it is a source of encouragement and strength to him to be made aware of it. When, on the other hand, the Representative fails to secure that confidence the sooner the scene of his labours is changed, the better.

In the early part of the year I had the pleasure of accompanying my friend and neighbour, Mr. J. H.

Batty, to the coffee plantations of the firm of Messrs. Miller Brothers, six or seven miles from Cape Coast. It was a great sight to see so many thousands of magnificent trees promising a rich harvest. We have sometimes been asked if it is not possible to improve the climatic conditions of the Colony. Our reply is: "Only by the cultivation of the land!" We sometimes imagine that if only the large tracts of land in that part of the world had not been so mercilessly depopulated by the greed of our forefathers there would to-day be a comparative struggle for existence, and the native, who now obtains his food with the least possible exertion, would have been compelled to cultivate the land. Were but one-half of the Colony under cultivation we might not unreasonably expect a happier condition of things than we observe at present.

It is quite true that we occasionally console ourselves with the reflection that the mortality among Europeans is not as great to-day as it was a hundred years ago. This is partly due to the fact that the physicians are more familiar with the symptoms of fever, and also with the necessary remedies. Again, in the principal Coast towns the Government has completed a system of drainage, and some of the towns are favoured with public scavengers. The vigilant eye of the Nuisance Inspector is constantly upon us, and we ourselves have been served with a summons for allowing a few weeds to grow in our compounds. But all these improvements are but a "drop in the bucket." Undoubtedly it is the duty of all law-abiding citizens to observe decency and order. But it is vain to dream of effecting a visible improvement in the climate when we have the dense, impenetrable, malarial-laden bush both in and around our towns. The prevailing land breeze neutralises our best hygienic efforts, and the result is that the European inhales malarial poison, in small or large quantities, the whole year round : even the natives themselves are not acclimatised.

We should rejoice to see more extensive tracts of land flourishing as coffee or cocoa plantations. The pioneers in this work have been the natives themselves—perhaps we ought to say the West Indian negroes. But the native grower, as a rule, has not understood the value of "cleaning" his land. He is now beginning to realise that the plantations of the firm just mentioned, and of the Government, repay the outlay involved in "grubbing" and "hoeing" foreign roots in the corresponding finer production of berries. I once felt quite complimented when visiting the plantation of a native friend, on hearing the owner say, "You see, I have taken your advice, and have dug up all old roots, and am keeping my land clean." The result was gratifying to both. My friend was also unconsciously conferring a benefit on his fellows generally by removing that which contributes to disease and death.

Another Gold Coast industry must here be mentioned. I refer to the extensive trade in mahogany.

THE BEACH AT AXIM, WITH MAHOGANY LOGS.

[To face page 160.

The pioneer in this industry, Mr. Clinton, of Axim, I met on my first voyage to Africa. He was most enthusiastic about the venture in mahogany logs. It was then the season of Christmas, and the reference to "logs" suggested the Yule log, and I marvelled greatly that a log could be of so much commercial value. But I was to learn that a mahogany log was in reality a huge baulk of timber, and therefore a valuable item in a ship's cargo. I have before me as I write the sketch of one which measures forty-one and a half feet in length, and forty by thirty-six inches on the sides, and weighs eight tons, five hundredweight. The brokers describe it as a "perfect log." The export in this trade increased from six thousand feet in 1890 to five million feet in 1894.

The pages of this book have hitherto been preserved from West Coast "yarns," so that I feel justified in introducing one here. The reader will imagine it is far-fetched. I can only say that it was related to me in perfect sincerity by one on whose veracity I could depend. Moreover, my experience of West Africa warrants my acceptance of the story A trader, accompanied by a gang of Kru boys, made a journey in search of mahogany trees, when a boa constrictor was suddenly discovered—quite torpid. The gallants begged permission to kill the reptile; this was, of course, readily granted. A post-mortem examination revealed the fact that the last haul made by the boa consisted of four

M

or five ducks and as many fowls, one only of which appeared to be in process of digestion. Now all Kru boys are of a decidedly economical turn of mind: moreover, they are not squeamish in articles of diet. I need say no more but allow imagination to fill in the rest. I am here reminded that I once possessed a horse in Africa—not a very valuable animal, certainly. I paid £7 for it without harness. After three months of faithful service it died of fever. A spot was selected for its grave. My economical Kru boy suggested that if only he could be permitted to take home one of the legs he and his friends would be able to make a feast. Permission was not given.

Missionaries engaged at the Gold Coast have the privilege of paying an occasional visit to a region in the neighbourhood of Accra, dignified by the name of "the mountains." It was not, however, until I was well advanced in my fifth year that I availed myself of this privilege. After ministering to my colleague, Mr. Arthur Hall, and to myself during simultaneous attacks of fever, my wife was strongly advised to take a trip to Aburi; we were assured that we should find the air delightfully cool and clear.

Calling at Christiansborg Castle to pay our respects to the Governor, we had the advice confirmed by His Excellency in a most practical manner. The private rooms at the sanatorium, the loan of two hammocks, and a supply of wraps and medical comforts were forthwith placed at our disposal. What further inducement did we need? A journey of twenty-six miles took us to Aburi. After having been so long accustomed to the wildest confusion in the "bush," which furnished an illustration of "the struggle for existence," it seemed most wonderful to find ourselves in full view of a large plot of ground carefully cleared, with a mighty silk-cotton tree one hundred and seventy feet high standing in the centre, "the survival of the fittest." Around the house, which was to be our home for a fortnight, we found neat beds of English and tropical flowers; and surrounding these were thousands of young and vigorous coffee and cocoa plants, cultivated by the Government with the view of encouraging industry among the natives. The curator was able to supply us with English vegetables: so that we felt quite at home. Our one regret was that we were not in our own house, where we might redeem the time by freely carrying on our work.

We found our mission sanatorium, which was built by the direction of the Committee some years previously: but most unfortunately it was in close proximity to a crowd of unwholesome native huts. The approach to it was most inconvenient. The fact that we had to pass through a back street was not so objectionable as were the odours arising therefrom; these would greatly minimise the benefits to be derived from this lovely hill country, which boasts of an altitude of 1,400 feet and of a temperature of 52° during the nights of the cold season.

After we had been at Aburi a few days the Governor, with a number of officers, and about 200 Houssa soldiers, made a halt at Government House, on his way to the Croboe Mount, about forty miles farther. Reports had reached Accra to the effect that the Croboes were seizing helpless strangers and taking their lives in order to observe their pagan customs. It was the intention of Sir Brandford Griffith to put a stop to these horrible customs, which were the cause of a hundred murders annually. Furnishing us with the necessary carriers, His Excellency very kindly invited us to accompany the expedition as far as to Akropong, a town of considerable importance twelve miles nearer to the notorious mount. At Akropong the natives, under king and chiefs, mustered in great force to do homage to Her Majesty's representative. It was estimated that seven thousand men, young and old, had possessed themselves of almost every conceivable form of firearm, from the eleven-and-threepenny gas-piped barrel to the Martini-Henri rifle. The sound of the firing was perfectly deafening. The king came in his war dress, thereby signifying that he was perfectly willing to go to the help of Her Majesty against the fierce Croboes. In the afternoon the Governor returned the visit, and made it very clear to his hearers that the cruel customs

Palaver at Akropong. Houssa Soldiers "at ease."

[To face page 164.

would be stopped by the strong arm of the Government. Late in the afternoon we took leave of His Excellency, and returned to Aburi, anxious to hear the result of the expedition. A few days later, during which many uncomfortable rumours were abroad, the company returned, and we were devoutly thankful to hear that the mission had been most successful. His Excellency said, "We gave due notice to the people to take away their household goods, and we had everything connected with the abominable practices placed in a heap, together with a great quantity of human bones and skulls—one apparently of a child of two years of age. We then had kerosene oil poured upon the whole, and I struck a match and set fire to it; and the flames seemed to come down and lick up the accursed things."

Croboe Mount is about forty miles beyond Aburi, and only a short distance from Kpong, a most promising Mission station on the river Volta. It has long since become too small to hold the tribe, which is now extending along the plain. The mount was for the most part kept sacred, as a residence for girls of the age of fourteen years and upwards. As many as 4,700 found their way there during 1891. The girls usually remained on the mount for a year or eighteen months, under the care of priests and priestesses. Previous to sending a damsel to the mount, the friends were in the habit of slaughtering a number of sheep; the number slain was supposed to be proportionate to the wealth of the family, which was often put to great inconvenience in order to keep up appearances. (The Acting Colonial Secretary informed me that the establishment cost £20,000 annually to maintain.) The fat of the slaughtered sheep was placed upon the head of the young lady, who was required to wear a curiously-shaped hat while she went through the test of walking over very steep slippery slabs of stone. In the event of the hat falling from her head, the unfortunate girl was sent back to her family in great disgrace. Those who passed the test were expected to wear the strange ornament during the whole of their term of residence.

The Lady Superior held herself quite aloof from the sterner sex. It was said that she was dedicated to the work in her infancy, and at no period of her life had she so much as touched a male. Indeed, until the soldiers, in carrying out the Governor's orders, conducted the old lady out of her house, no man had darkened her doorway. The pagans quite expected to see the soldiers fall down dead during their daring act. The house, however, was doomed, and shortly afterwards was in ruins.

I took considerable pains to ascertain from the officers, both European and native, some particulars of the barbarous customs. As far as I could understand, the girls were dedicated by their friends to a particular fetish : either the *Otufu* or *Deepo*, at whose festival the most disgusting scenes were enacted; the *Nadu* and *Koko Nadu*, at whose festival the fame and glory of ancestors were sung, and this, in stimulating to deeds of daring, often led to brutality and robbery; and the *Koto Kru*. In the latter festival only *murderers* could take part—that is to say, only those who could produce either the top of a skull or the thigh bones of men whom they had murdered, were allowed to take part in the Koto Kru "custom." A few weeks previously four men and a *boy* were apprehended on a charge of murder. We understood from His Excellency that, in the event of conviction, the adult criminals would be executed on the fetish mount. A few months later the men were hanged in public.

A part of one of the skulls found at the Croboe charnel-house found its way to Accra, and is now in my possession. I am assured that the pagans in celebrating their orgies would use it as a wine-cup. Our senior native superintendent, the Rev. A. W. Parker, was of opinion that this skull has been used for an ornament for a king's "tom-tom" or "stool." I have repeatedly seen similar decorations in other parts of the Colony.

On the occasion of the Governor's visit, a new king—one who had had the privilege of Christian training by the Basle Missionaries—was placed upon the much-coveted stool. His Excellency required an assurance that the king would exert himself to put down the horrible practices, and at the same time he assured His Majesty of the assistance of the Government. In proof of this assurance, a company of one hundred Houssas, with an English officer, was left in charge of the place, with instructions to put down any attempt at reviving the customs. I subsequently learnt that some very shocking discoveries were made in the immediate neighbourhood, and that the people still had a hankering after the old mode of life.

We felt thankful that the Government had—to use a figure—manacled the sanguinary wretches. But at the same time we were convinced that only a superhuman power could change their dispositions.

CHAPTER XI

THE DRINK TRAFFIC—OUR ATTITUDE AS A CHURCH TOWARDS THE QUESTION—SUGGESTIONS TO THE GOVERNMENT—RECKLESS TRAVELLING—HIS EXCELLENCY THE GOVERNOR AND THE COLONIAL SECRETARY TESTIFY TO THE VALUE OF MISSION WORK—PROPOSAL TO ESTABLISH GIRLS' BOARDING SCHOOL AT ABURI—PRACTICAL SUPPORT OF THE HOME GOVERNMENT

TOWARDS the latter part of the year the patriots of Cape Coast decided to arrange a purely native entertainment. Every syllable of every song was rendered in the vernacular; the dresses of the artistes were certainly made after the fashions of the country, though I have no doubt the material itself for the most part came from Manchester.

One item of the programme necessitated the adoption of an English dress—for the actor was supposed to represent an English father. A translation of that pathetic ballad, "Father, come home!" was sung by a little girl. At the end of the first verse, a youth dressed in ragged attire, with a battered silk hat, came reeling on to the platform. I naturally felt very much ashamed at the thought that to obtain an illustration of the evils of the drink traffic the actors found it necessary to personate an

Englishman. I felt still more ashamed that the acting of a song which represents the anguish of so many broken hearts in this country should have provoked only mirth in the audience. And yet their very ignorance conveyed a grain of comfort to me; for I was thereby convinced that they were not familiar with—they had happily been spared—the sorrows that had blighted so many homes in England.

About the same time, as far as I can remember, I was invited to speak at a meeting of the Good Templars of the town of Cape Coast. One of my native colleagues also gave a Temperance address. I shall not soon forget the earnestness with which he exhorted his hearers to fight the gigantic demon strong drink. "For," said he, "unless we do put forth our best efforts in this direction, there is a danger of becoming as drunken as the people of England." This was a rather startling way of putting the case, but it was decidedly refreshing, as I remembered that there were so many in England who appear to be under the impression that whole territories are being depopulated by the importation of spirits.

The sentiment expressed by my colleague was forceful, but I unhesitatingly repeat and endorse it. Long before this period I had formed a Band of Hope in connection with our day school, so as to lend a hand in preventing the rising generation from becoming "as drunken as the people of England." It should be a comfort to friends of Africa to know that the evils of the drink traffic are much less serious at the Gold Coast than appears to be the case in some parts of the Dark Continent. Concerning the Gold Coast and the drink traffic, I am thankful to be able to say : First, that the drink traffic does not tend to poverty ; this may be due to the fact that poverty is entirely unknown in that highly favoured land. Second, that it does not bring in its train the untold social misery with which we are so sadly familiar in this country ; but then, of course, the conditions of social life are totally different. Third, that it does not tend to the perpetration of crime. A friend of mine, a most ardent temperance reformer, was appointed District Commissioner of Cape Coast a few months prior to my first year of residence. At the end of his first term of service he took the opportunity to write to a temperance newspaper in this country to say that the friends of temperance would be glad to know that the ravages of the drink traffic were not as serious at the Gold Coast as was generally supposed. Out of the hundreds of cases tried in his court during the twelve months not one was traceable to the abuse of strong drink.

I have not the slightest hesitation in saying that instances of drunkenness are comparatively rare in the streets of Cape Coast. The principal sufferers by the traffic are the fishermen, who are engaged in transferring cargo from ocean vessels to the shore ; and other pagans at their festivals. It is suggested that those addicted to strong drink quietly withdraw from public thoroughfares, and thus escape the eye of the European. This may be so. But in however favourable a light the consequences of the traffic may be regarded, I should by no means relax my effort for its prohibition. I would gladly stop it at once if it were in my power to do so. And this because the native who abstains is infinitely superior to the man who indulges. I can, of course, give no scientific opinion upon the subject, but I have the conviction that the spirits, which, by the way, are manufactured on the Continent and America, are injurious to the natives.

How is the drink question to be dealt with? As a Mission we have introduced stern measures to mark our disapproval of the trade. No member of our Church is permitted to hold a licence for the sale of spirits. Some of our people have thus been compelled to sacrifice a considerable portion of their income in order to retain their connection with us; others have been compelled to sacrifice the privilege of Church membership. This measure is no doubt exceedingly drastic, and I frankly confess that I, for one, could not be a party to similar legislation for this country. But then the legislation suitable to this country cannot always be adapted to meet the requirements of heathen populations. Although we have the greatest respect for the intelligence of the educated natives of the Gold

Coast, we have to bear in mind the fact that this proportion is infinitesimal compared with the great mass whom we must regard as children in understanding. And then we who have passed this legislation—and natives have been decidedly in the majority at our annual Synods—have the conviction that the most that can be said in favour of the "trade spirits" is that they are useful to the naturalist for the preservation of specimens, and to the Government as a source of revenue. I have no doubt that our Synod's attitude towards the whole question accounts for the comparative sobriety of the tribes in the Colony.

But although quite prepared to defend stringent measures by an ecclesiastical body, we would by no means require a political government to make our natives total abstainers by "Act of Parliament." We, as a Church, legislate for that portion of the community desiring to be associated with us. But the Government has to legislate for all sorts and conditions of men. We would respectfully suggest to the Government that the import duties on spirits be considerably increased, so as to minimise the quantity imported. But at the same time we cannot expect our Government to introduce a scale of charges so as to render the introduction of spirits prohibitive, while France on the one side of us and Germany on the other are admitting precisely the same article at nominal rates. For this would only encourage smuggling. Nor can we expect our

Colonial Office to successfully negotiate with the other Governments interested in West Africa, for the greatest jealousy prevails among them. No; just as an independent British public succeeded in convincing the powers of Europe of this nation's disinterested attitude towards the persecuted Armenians, so it seems to me to be the duty of independent philanthropic bodies in the European countries represented in West Africa to approach their respective Governments with a view to bringing about uniformity of action in the interests of West African humanity.

One other word respecting the native races and the liquor question. We all know that the followers of Mohammed are required to be total abstainers. And we have sometimes heard it suggested that Mohammedans are much more sober than are the Christians. It is somewhat remarkable that I have seen a greater number of drunkards among Mohammedans than among Christians. To which I expect to hear the retort, " Yes, but there are Mohammedans *and* Mohammedans !" Quite so, as also there are Christians *and* Christians. In the whole of my experience at the Gold Coast I had occasion to " discipline " only one member of our Church for drunkenness, and that member had become intoxicated by the native palm wine.

And now I have a confession to make. We actually indulged in the luxury of a tennis court at the Mission House. It came about in this way :

Our friend the Colonial Surgeon of Cape Coast took a great interest in the recreation, and not merely invited but urged his friends to the hospital court. He explained that it was quite against his professional interests to do so, inasmuch as the exercise contributed to the health of those who otherwise might become his patients. The court was so extensively patronised that we had qualms of conscience in imposing on our friend's good nature. We had a respectable lawn of our own; and so, with a very little labour, we were able to convert it into a tennis court. I have really introduced the subject in order to say that moderate exercise in this direction is decidedly beneficial to one's health. Care must, however, be taken not to indulge to the extent of over-exertion, or the result may prove as disastrous as is the absence of all exercise. As Cape Coast is so near the equator the tennis hour was from five to six P.M. all the year round; and this hour, by the way, was the only hour during the day which was devoted to recreation.

But we had also entertained the idea of allowing the lads residing with us the opportunity of playing the favourite game. For by this time some twenty young people had been received into our home. We had arranged that the parents and friends should supply the necessary food and also furnish the cost of education. Our reason for undertaking this branch of missionary work is obvious. We have already hinted that some of the "homes" in the district were exceedingly dirty. It was John Wesley who first insisted on the principle that "cleanliness is next to godliness." We therefore regarded it as a special duty of ours to instil principles of cleanliness into the minds of our boys. They were accordingly supplied with whitewash, paint, and pictures, in order to make the rooms placed at their disposal as neat and attractive as possible. In one room might have been observed a "Plan for keeping the room nice." This was arranged by the lads themselves. The lady of the house, who was a great favourite with our young friends, paid a visit each morning to the rooms to see that all was in order. This attention was heartily appreciated, and when friendly help with needle and thread was required, they knew where they might obtain assistance.

It is scarcely necessary to say that with such a band of youthful spirits about us we rarely ever lacked entertainment. Occasionally we found it necessary to quell a little disturbance at an unseemly hour of the night. But we were quite prepared to excuse a little noise, for we had good reason to believe that even with such a small company there was the prospect of developing manly characters. It was customary to summon the lads to the dining-room at 7 A.M. and at 9 P.M. for family prayer. The portion of Scripture was selected for them and was read by one of the lads in turn. Some of the hymns sung on these occasions will ever be associated in my mind with the lads. We look back with great pleasure to the time we spent with our "family." Most of the members are scattered about in various parts of the Colony, filling positions of responsibility with satisfaction to their employers and with credit to themselves.

I may here, perhaps, mention the fact that our industrial department executed two important orders during the year. One was to build a hand-lorry. Our carpenter was enabled to turn the hub and to make the felloes and spokes satisfactorily, but our blacksmith was not sufficiently skilful to weld the iron tires. The latter were therefore obtained from Liverpool. But the department naturally felt very proud when the order was completed. The second order was to re-paint and re-paper the room of our Irish neighbour. This was a more difficult undertaking, as none of us had used a paperhanger's brush. But we conquered, and all concerned were fairly satisfied.

Among the visitors to the school was the Chief Justice of the Colony, Sir J. T. Hutchinson, who was good enough to express his pleasure with our progress. This testimony was greatly appreciated, from the fact that Sir Joseph was regarded throughout the Colony as an authority on schools. We were also honoured with a visit from Dr. Ingham, Bishop of Sierra Leone. The Bishop very kindly gave an address to the senior division, and was greatly pleased with the manner in which the address was reproduced in writing : an evidence both of the intelligence and attention of the scholars, particularly when it is remarked that they were unaware till after the address was given that they would be required to reduce the same to writing.

The annual Government exhibition of school handicrafts at Accra secured for us the approval of the Board of Education. Our boys won first and second prizes for joinery, smiths' work, and clay-modelling, and also a second prize for drawing. And as these were considered inadequate an extra grant of £5 was made by the Board to the school. We must admit that even these results do not speak volumes for our work, for scarcely any other school competed. Nevertheless, we were greatly encouraged. The humbler results of the girls' examination perhaps testified to equally great diligence, for they had had to compete with girls who for some years had been under the tuition of the devoted nuns and German lady missionaries.

The District Report for the year 1892 says:—

"The Sunday schools have advanced rapidly: an increase of over two thousand scholars. It is hoped that this will be a permanent work.

"The day schools have an increase of more than eight hundred scholars. These schools are practically independent of the Missionary Society's financial assistance. It is instructive to notice in the most recently published Government Report on education that in the Basle Mission schools there are fifty-nine girls to every hundred boys; the Roman

Catholics have twenty-eight; the Government twenty-five; but our own schools have only eleven girls to every hundred boys!

"The work of our Technical Institution exceeds our most sanguine expectations. At the end of the year we had thirty-eight lads learning useful trades. We hope to make the number up to fifty, and we are sanguine enough to expect the services of an English mechanic to superintend the work. We are earnestly desirous that youths from the various circuits in the District shall avail themselves of the privileges of our institution."

A somewhat amusing little incident occurred at the annual school examination. Our scholars, for some inexplicable reason, invariably pronounce the letter "u" as "e," and will insist, for example, in calling "butter" "better." The senior scholars were asked to name the principal seaports of England. One little lad thought of "Hull." But in consequence of the difficulty just mentioned the examiner did not recognise the name, and somewhat absent-mindedly asked in which part of England "Hell" was. Our young friends sometimes find that the English language is to them what an African once assured me the native language would be to me—"a verra deeficult language to pronounce properly!"

In October I performed a record journey from Appam to Cape Coast—a distance of forty miles—

in twelve hours. I was returning from Accra overland when I received a telegram from my colleague to say that my wife was ill, not seriously, but that I had better hasten home. The telegram came into my hands just twenty-six hours after it was despatched from Cape Coast. The wording of the message was somewhat disquieting, and I feared that in that treacherous land there was ample time in twenty-six hours for more serious developments. Hence the reckless rate of travelling. I found on reaching home that matters had assumed a serious aspect, for my medical friend had, for twenty-four hours, found it necessary to be in almost constant attendance. But, as is often the case in West Africa, when once the critical stage was passed convalescence was rapid.

At the end of the year the head of the "paternal" Government very kindly invited us to spend a few days at Christiansborg Castle. The old Danish fort proved a convalescent home to many a Government official during the residence of Sir Brandford Griffith, whose interest in the health and comfort of the European residents was proverbial.

The annual missionary meeting at Accra was presided over by his Excellency the Governor, supported by the Colonial Secretary, the Honourable F. M. Hodgson, C.M.G., and other officers. We very gratefully noted the testimony of the Government to the value of the Mission work in the Colony. Our suggestion respecting the establishment of a girls' boarding school at Aburi was made public, and we were assured of the practical sympathy of the Government in this undertaking.

The following paragraphs are culled from the Report of the year:—

"The superintendent of the Cape Coast Sunday schools reports numerical increases, progress in scriptural knowledge, and influence for good upon the lives of heathen children. By means of the Fanti singing band the Gospel in song has been proclaimed through the lips of children to many outside the pale of the Church. The influence of the work has been felt at Abura, a village three miles away; at the request of the villagers we have recently opened a school with a hundred and twenty-six children in attendance. Already it has been the means of leading two women from heathenism to Christianity.

"A fear is expressed that our numerical increase may ultimately prove costly. Our Sunday school anniversaries are in danger of lowering the standard of Christianity. If it is a fact that the processions headed by drum and fife bands ultimately lead to the ball-room, the heathen dance, and other worldly amusements, there can be no question as to what our action must be. In our anxiety for numerical success we must not encourage methods which, however proper in themselves, create a relish for unholy and degrading pleasures."

The next paragraph is of pathetic interest to the

present writer, inasmuch as it was originally penned by a young native minister, who had scarcely completed it when he was seized with an illness from which he did not recover. All who knew him honour the memory of the Rev. Isaac Anaman, who, in addition to the endowment of natural gifts, was a most conscientious worker among his fellows, and was held in the highest esteem by his European and native fellow-workers. These facts will add to the interest on the part of the reader, particularly as the Report testifies to the power of the Gospel of Christ :—

"The year has been one of the most glorious with which the Head of the Church has been pleased to favour us. We thankfully report progress all along the line. The attendance at the Sunday and week-night services at Elmina has greatly increased. Sekundi is also making headway. Chama still sorely needs the services of a thoroughly competent assistant minister. The town is growing in importance. At Brenu Akyinm' the natives have been made to feel that the world has been turned upside down. Three Fetish chief priests have been led to Christianity—we trust, to Christ. The converts were earnestly entreated by their relatives and fellow-townsmen to return to their former craft, sums of money were offered to tempt them, but to no purpose. Persuasions and threatenings having failed, recourse was had to persecutions ; and our friends have had to suffer and patiently endure, not only the trial of cruel mockings, reproaches, and reviling, but, moreover, of bodily assault and buffetings from even their own relatives. We have had the joy of baptizing two of these, the third has left the neighbourhood for a short time. Great service has been rendered to the Church through the public testimony borne by the converts to the power of the Gospel, and also by the fearless manner in which they have disclosed the tricks of the Fetish priestcraft. A talisman—highly prized as the insignia of the priest's office—was handed to us on the day of the public profession. We propose building a chapel here, the chief and head men having promised us land for the purpose."

The superintendent of the Anamabu circuits reports:—

"At Abiadzi, a little lad of twelve years has been the means of bringing eighteen converts to Christ. At Gyirankuma, one of the worst characters in the town has been admitted into Church membership; after having devoted his life to idol worship, his eyes have been opened to its folly, and he has decided to live for God."

From Winnebah we learn that a Fetish priest and several adherents renounced their paganism. We refer to these incidents, for, as we have elsewhere explained, the Fetish priest is usually above the average native in intelligence. His renunciation means the sacrifice of considerable income;

and is therefore a striking testimony to the reality of the man's conversion.

In the same circuit, discipline was exercised upon those who engaged in the sale of spirits. The effect was salutary: other members and officers of the Church were led to reflection, and to the subsequent abandonment of the trade.

Under the heading of Dix Cove Day Schools we read:—

"In consequence of the flourishing timber industry there is a growing desire for education. This probably accounts, to some extent, for the liberality of the chiefs in this circuit in providing for the stipends of the teachers employed at some of the new stations; while every minister is anxious to see our young people civilised, the end we have in view is the salvation of every scholar. At Axim, Dix Cove, Busuia, Princes, Essiamah, Kikam, Attuabu, Beyin, Egyambra, Cape Three Points, and Akwadah, the chiefs have either paid our superintendent sums of £20 or £25, or have pledged themselves to maintain the teachers. In response to an urgent appeal a provisional school was opened at Half Assine, the chiefs readily paying £25 for the experiment. Prior to the superintendent's visit the natives had erected a substantial bamboo shed, and had reserved the best part of the town for the Mission. At the opening of the schools, the pagan chiefs publicly implored the ministers to pray for a blessing upon themselves and their people."

It may be mentioned that the total amount raised in the District for the year, including the Government grant in aid of education, was £5,079.

The missionary meeting held in connection with the annual Synod was addressed by the genial and brotherly Canon Taylor Smith, now Bishop of Sierra Leone. The Chaplain and the Assistant Chaplain of the Colony also supported the chairman, who was a large-hearted member of the Church of England.

At the close of the Synod we welcomed a new missionary worker, the Rev. G. C. Main, of Didsbury College, to whom was specially entrusted the charge of the Institution for the Training of Native Catechists and Teachers. For reasons already given we experienced a great difficulty in securing an adequate number of young men for the Institution. The few who availed themselves of the advantages greatly appreciated the painstaking labour of the new principal. Mr. Main also devoted attention to the elementary schools and the book depot.

In March we went home on furlough. Our one anxiety concerning the Gold Coast work was the establishment of a girls' school and sanatorium.

We had stated our need to the members of the Legislative Council, and had intimated that, although we were convinced that the Missionary Committee would support us to the best of its ability, yet we were equally convinced that we should be unable to command sufficient funds to enable us to carry out our plans. A building, together with furniture and school apparatus such as we required, would entail the cost of £1,800. We ventured to appeal to the Colonial Government for one half of that amount. The members of the Council, both official and unofficial, promised to give the matter their most favourable consideration.

The following is a sketch of the scheme submitted to the Missionary Committee and to our friends in England :—

"I. THE OBJECT.

" We propose the establishment of an Institution which shall serve a double purpose :—

" 1. As an EDUCATIONAL CENTRE (day and boarding), to include—

>Elementary Education,
>Advanced Education,
>Training in Domestic Economy,
>Industrial Education.

" 2. As a SANATORIUM—
>For Christian workers, ministerial and lay, in connection with the Mission,
"For the European ladies of the Colony.
"(A) Girls' School : 1, Educational need.

"(i) Although our Mission has been nearly sixty years in existence, there is, nevertheless, a lamentable absence of refining influence in domestic life. Woman is by no means considered the equal—

[*To face page* 186.

A FAITHFUL FRIEND IN THE HOUR OF SICKNESS.

rather the slave—to man. It follows from this that the family life is very far from ideal.

"(ii) The present system of education is inefficient, being only of the barest elementary character. Our boys and girls are miscellaneously grouped together, which, it will be understood, is most injurious to the morals of the young people. In the absence of European lady workers we are doing nothing towards making better wives and mothers. Our girls are simply taught to read and write, but are not lifted above their present surroundings.

"(iii) The education given in England—which at best, can be given to only a few—is totally unsuited to local requirements. An English education is for English people, surrounded by English environment. It is needless to point out the difference between the two countries in the matter of food, dress, manners and customs in social life, the position of woman as wife and mother. An African girl trained in England on her return finds, to her sorrow, that she has to descend from her lofty position. She has to exchange the drawing-room for the swish building; refinement and the restrictions of English society for the questionable freedom of native life. The result sometimes is that her last state is worse than the first. Corresponding advantages furnished in the district would be less costly, and would also benefit a much larger number of girls; and by keeping those in training in touch with their families it would subject them to no violent changes, and would greatly benefit the homes from which the girls come, and so tend to elevate the entire family and the class.

"(iv) There is great need of female workers in our Church. If this is felt in England, with all its advantages, how much more in Africa! In 1842-3 Mrs. Watkins—the wife of a missionary—conducted a girls' school in Cape Coast with seventy-nine pupils. As a result of this undertaking a number of sturdy Christian women subsequently became workers in the Church, acting as class-leaders, etc., and many of them married the best members of our Church. Experience proves that native women as class-leaders for women are to be preferred to men.

"No corresponding work having been done in recent years, there is a paucity of female helpers and an entire absence of female teachers in our day schools. This is having a prejudicial effect upon our Church life, and greatly limiting the sphere of Christian influence.

"(v) At the present time our people are in a dilemma: they have either to neglect their girls, or send them to Roman Catholic Schools. Now, there is, from the nature of things, no *home life* connected with the Roman Catholic Mission; but at the present time there are ten Roman Catholic sisters in the district. It is, therefore, not surprising that the daughters of our people are sent to them to be trained. Our leading laymen have confessed with sorrow that, unless Protestant sisters come to the rescue, there is no other course open to them."

The next paragraph dealt with the lamentable disproportion of girls attending our day schools, as compared with the schools of other Missions.

"(B) Industrial Training.

"(i) At the present time there are two classes of females in the district—the "lady" and the "cloth woman." The former is supposed to be "educated," and adopts English dress, and is above menial occupation; the latter is generally, though not necessarily, illiterate, and consequently becomes the drudge.

"(ii) The great success which has followed our efforts to combine industrial work with our boys' school at Cape Coast convinces us that we can in like manner teach girls useful occupations, and thus put within their reach the means of self support.

"(iii) The Government is beginning to employ girls in the Telegraph Department. In addition to preparing them for this, we might teach laundry-work, nursing, hygiene, and dressmaking."

The next sub-section related to the need of a Sanatorium, as evidenced by the interruptions in the work on account of the ill-health of the missionaries.

". . . . Aburi, where the Sanatorium would be established, is used by the Government as a health resort for officers, and by the Basle Missionary Society for similar purposes. It is 1,400 feet above the sea level, and but one day's journey from Accra.

The Government is proposing to open the country by laying a line of railway to this centre. The temperature is delightfully cool. During our stay there last August the thermometer registered during the night 51°. At the same time we derived very great benefit."

The following section dealt with the *modus operandi*, and the expected ultimate results of the undertaking, into which we need not here enter.

The practical proof of the interest of the Government in the undertaking will be gathered from the following :—

"Downing Street,
"*October* 23, 1893.

"Sir,—I am directed by the Marquess of Ripon to acknowledge the receipt of your letter of 17th instant, asking what decision has been taken with regard to your proposal to establish an Institution for the higher education and domestic training of native girls at the Gold Coast Colony.

"In reply I am to acquaint you that Lord Ripon has informed the officer administering the Government that he concurs in the opinion expressed by Sir B. Griffith that every encouragement should be given to the spread of education at the Gold Coast, especially among the female population, and that your proposal appears to his Lordship to be deserving of support.

"He has therefore authorised Mr. Hodgson to propose to the Legislative Council to vote a grant towards the cost of the Institution, on the understanding, as suggested by Sir B. Griffith, that an equal amount has been obtained otherwise, and that under no circumstances will the grant of the Government be increased at a subsequent period.

"The grant is to be limited to £900, *i.e.* 50 per cent. of the amount estimated by you as the cost of the building and furniture,

"I am, etc.,
"(Signed) JOHN BRAMSTON."

Our Committee generously sanctioned the expenditure of £550. £100 was subsequently voted from the profits of our Gold Coast Book Depot; and £250 was obtained from personal friends and those interested in Missions.

I have heard of a tax collector who once was kicked by a horse so that his jaw was broken. But the curious part of the incident was that "it didn't hurt his *cheek!*" I have ever envied that man the latter part of the experience. For I am bound to confess that the result of my begging expedition forced from me the remark of the unjust steward of old, "to beg I am ashamed!"

CHAPTER XII

THE STEAMSHIP "CALABAR"—ADVANCE IN SHIPPING ACCOMMODATION—DIFFICULTIES IN NEGOTIATING LAND QUESTIONS WITH THE UNSOPHISTICATED AFRICAN—A PLAGUE OF LOCUSTS—"LIBERTY, FRATERNITY, EQUALITY"—THE GOLD COAST BOARD OF EDUCATION—DIFFICULTIES IN BUILDING—THE TRANSPORT QUESTION—KRU BOYS TO THE RESCUE

THE district again suffered a loss, in the transference to the home work of a missionary of experience. Our old friend Mr. Price was forbidden by Dr. Gage Brown to return to the Coast. At my suggestion Rev. W. F. Somerville, of Richmond College, volunteered to fill the vacancy. The missionary designate had spent his whole life at school, first as pupil, latterly as a master; and was thus well qualified to occupy the position to which he was specially appointed, viz., the oversight of the day and Sunday schools of the district, a work which he anticipated with the greatest possible pleasure.

The arrival of a son and heir in our home necessitated my wife's remaining in England for a time. Hence it came to pass that in November I found myself a single man, on board the dear delightful old sea-tub, the s.s. "Calabar." Messrs. Elder, Dempster and Co. have made enormous strides in their shipping business during the last ten years. At the beginning of '88 the "Calabar" was certainly among the best of the Company's fleet; a passenger would not have minded waiting a week in order to secure a passage in her. To-day the same passenger would gladly wait a week to avoid her; and this, not so much from the fact that she is invariably on the "parliamentary" run, but because almost all her "step"-sisters are decidedly more attractive.

Despite the discomforts of the passage I had one compensation, inasmuch as I had the pleasure of a sight of Bathurst. This is, I believe, the only town on the coast—at least as far as British possessions are concerned—which boasts of stone pavements to some of its streets. And they are sorely needed: for the town is built on a sandbank—and the discomfort in walking through the streets without a pavement can be better imagined than described. My stay at Bathurst was made most agreeable by the kind attention of the Honourable Mr. Forster and Mr. Topp, natives of the town. On Sunday I had the privilege of preaching at our church. As I looked around I questioned the wisdom of adorning the pillars of the gallery with marble slabs, erected to the memory of our missionaries who had died in the town. I did not wonder that such a sight had had a depressing effect upon young men coming out from England for their first tour.

From a political point of view it seems rather odd that this little Colony, so circumscribed by the French, and so useless, apparently, to the English crown, is not handed over to our neighbours; but then, I am not a politician. On higher grounds I should like to see Britain in possession of the whole of Africa; of which more hereafter.

What promised to be an almost interminable voyage did eventually come to an end! The most noteworthy event of it was the birth of a little negro as we neared Cape Coast. The mother came aboard at Dix Cove on Christmas afternoon; the little one arrived during the night; a few hours later I saw the mother ashore, looking as though the little incident was by no means extraordinary in her experience. A very brief stay was made at Cape Coast, in order to make arrangements for the approaching Synod; and then Mr. Hall and I went on to Accra for Aburi, with a view to securing a site and laying the foundation-stones of our new building. The first was by no means a light undertaking. Just the site we wanted could not be had for love or money. And for the next best site a fabulous sum was demanded. There are untold thousands of acres of land lying perfectly idle, and perfectly valueless except for the palm trees, whose commercial value is estimated at a shilling a-piece—which might be put to good account by merchants and others, were it not for the over-reaching greed of the owners. A coloured solicitor, whom I consulted respecting the title deeds, said, "You will have observed, I suppose, that your 'poor benighted African' is quite capable of taking care of himself when driving a bargain?' Indeed I had. The exceptions to the rule, I always find, are when he attempts too much. Shylock would sometimes blush for very shame. We were asked £300 for a piece of land the value of which, honestly, was not more than £30: of course we did not entertain the offer for a moment; but time was of great importance with us, and so we invested £25—a handsome sum of money—in securing suitable land, and speedily set to work.

We had decided that our ground floor should be of stone, and the superstructure of wood. The latter was fitted up in England, and sent out in various shipments. We were most fortunate in having the assistance of Mr. Halligey in superintending the construction in England, and of Mr. Hall's help in setting out the foundations. Our main building was 75 by 23 feet, with a verandah on all sides. The site selected was about eighteen miles from the sea-shore; but, looking towards the south-east, we could see for a distance of thirty miles, and with the aid of a telescope we easily distinguished the flags of steamers at anchor twenty miles away.

The lower parts of the wall up to the floor were thirty inches thick, and reminded one of the old abbey walls in England. Stone was very plentiful, and mortar everywhere under our very feet. It was necessary to exercise care that all woodwork was fixed in cement, for the white ant plays sad havoc with white pine, and has no objection to attacking the harder pine. I have, by the way, seen a thin shell removed, from what was supposed to be a pine beam, when it was discovered that in addition to the outer shell there were actually only the hard knots remaining. For water we did not lack. By a most extraordinary coincidence the Fetish swamp, to which reference is elsewhere made, contained as much water as we required during the lengthy building operations. But about the time that our need ceased, the supply also ceased; and I am not aware that any quantity has collected there since.

For the first three months we found employment for fifty pairs of hands. General factotum, carpenter, timekeeper, twelve masons, twenty-seven male labourers, and eight females—the latter being used as carriers. There was no lack of applicants for work. For several mornings some score or more of rejected candidates for employment returned to their homes wiser, but sadder. But this condition of things did not continue long. Money became decidedly too plentiful, notwithstanding the fact that to skilled labourers we paid only one-and-ninepence a day, and to ordinary labourers only eightpence. Cement and lime had to be fetched in fifty-pound loads from Accra—twenty-six miles away, which meant at least two shillings for porterage; and this, when work and money were scarce; the expense was considerably more when the male labourers were sent, or when any of our employees could afford to be independent.

On one occasion, when taking a photograph of the building operations, the sky became suddenly overcast with a swarm of locusts, which settling down cleared away every prospect of a corn harvest. I may here remark that, for several seasons in succession we were visited by this plague. On one occasion I passed a procession which thickly covered the ground for at least twenty yards on either side of the road, and stretched a distance of twenty miles: we had by this time cleared the land necessary for our requirements, and had planted it with Indian corn. It seems incredible, but it is nevertheless an absolute fact, that out of the thousands of stalks standing at six feet high, one, and one only, was passed by much to the amusement of our timekeeper; the rest were stripped of every vestige of a blade. I can offer no explanation; it is too much to suppose that they left that solitary stalk in derision. Possibly the order was given to "march," and thus it escaped by accident. It was quite pitiful to see some of the old women endeavouring to put down the scourge—their efforts were about as vain as would be the attempt to extinguish a conflagration with a drop of water.

As I saw the pitiless swarm I thought of the

words, "I will restore to you the years that the locust hath eaten . . . . My great army which I sent you."

In passing through the swarm I was struck with the fact that there were no dead bodies to be observed, although it was evident that many must have been killed by the foot of the pedestrian. I therefore killed one and watched the result. I soon observed that they were most voracious cannibals, for in an instant the body was torn apart by its hungry companions.

Our mode of travelling between Accra and Aburi was by means of a hand-cart. There was a plain of twenty miles to be crossed, with very little shelter from the sun's rays. The last four miles were on the ascent, one part of the journey being over an exceedingly rocky road. Once only did I succeed in doing the distance of twenty-six miles under six hours. I have been on the road at all hours of the day and night. To sit upright in a jolting car, even though protected from the sun by an umbrella and helmet, is not equally as comfortable as railway travelling in England; and night-travelling, though preferable, is attended with risks, inasmuch as the drowsy traveller is in danger of tumbling off the vehicle. On two occasions I have gratefully availed myself of the comfort derived from a couple of hours' sleep on the bench of the village blacksmith, "under the spreading tree," with the faithful labourers and the village goats and sheep as my companions.

It was necessary to take the journey a great many times during that first year. The Synod at Cape Coast—the circuit of Accra—and the affairs of the district generally, demanded attention. I find among my letters of that time more than one reference to the apostolic injunction: " If it be possible, as much as lieth in you, live peaceably with all men." The inference was, that there were occasions when St. Paul was forced to the conclusion that peace was not at all times possible. I must confess that I, once in a while, sheltered myself behind the Apostle's own example, and fought. I need not enter into details; suffice it to say, that instances occurred when my judgment in official matters ran counter to the wishes of those with whom I desired to be at peace. It seems necessary to make this statement, for the purpose of intimating that one was not in the habit of endorsing all that was seen or heard.

Among other matters discussed at the Synod was a request to establish missionary operations in the French Colony of the Ivory Coast. Had not a slight attack of fever laid me aside at an inconvenient time, I had intended visiting the Governor at Grand Bassam, in order to gain permission for the establishment of a school. On the voyage a few months previously, I had the pleasure of meeting a suave officer of the service—a perfect Frenchman—and I had gathered from him that such an institution would doubtless be hailed with satisfaction by his Excellency. I was not, however, sanguine of the success of my application, so that I was not altogether disappointed when, in reply, I was informed that only a graduate of a French university could be permitted to carry on such a work—in other words, "only Frenchmen need apply." But the irony of writing such a communication on official notepaper, with the well-known motto, "Liberty, Fraternity, Equality"! As I write I have before me a letter from one of our missionaries at Porto Novo, another French possession, in which I learn that the writer and his companion were ordered to accompany a police commissionaire and two gendarmes to the Governor, to answer for the heinous offence of having announced a public service *in English*. Our friends were given to understand that the use of the English language was forbidden in that Colony. The same law applies in the neighbouring German Colony. Our Missionary Society was, a few years ago, given notice to quit, unless, within a given period, a German teacher was substituted for the English teacher.

The reader who respects the patriotism of these nations, very naturally exclaims, "And why not?" To which we, who have resided at the Gold Coast, reply, "We are thankful to say that our Government permits the greatest possible freedom. Honest John Bull allows representatives of any nation under the sun the greatest liberty, and is afraid to trust no one!" While English merchants and missionaries in other colonies are greatly restricted, and are subjected to the serious inconvenience and annoyances, John Bull opens his arms and invites the foreign representatives to take every possible liberty with him and his property. We would that "Liberty, Fraternity, Equality," prevailed throughout the whole of the European possessions in Africa.

And now we were to suffer another loss in the removal of one who had become familiar with the country. Mr. Arthur Hall had indeed succeeded in completing two years of residence on his second tour, but had suffered so much that each of his medical attendants had strongly advised him not to return to the Coast.

Occasional residence at Accra, the seat of Government, gave me the opportunity of becoming acquainted with the natives, known as the Gâs. My friend Price, whose views, generally, were very pronounced, ever insisted that the tribe was the finest in the Colony, inasmuch as it had never suffered defeat by an enemy in warfare. I could never, however, quite see that the Accras were in any respect superior to the natives of the old capital. The "native quarters" of the town were, I am afraid, generations behind those of Cape Coast. And, what concerned me most, the natives were less enthusiastic in missionary enterprise than were the Fantis.

The same accident which befell ancient London

and opened the way for improved streets and sanitation also befell Accra in 1894. I find that in the first four months of that year no fewer than seventeen fires broke out, in each case among houses with thatched roofs. Extensive areas were thus ablaze. Some of the illiterate natives attributed the blame to the Governor, others charged the English police officers with being the cause of the calamity. On one occasion a procession of the gentler sex paraded the streets and gave vent to their feelings by chanting an impromptu song, accompanied by clapping of hands. On inquiry I learnt that they were abusing the king, as they suspected that he was guilty of playing into the hands of the Government. By some it was stated that the later fires were the work of a maniacal incendiary, who considered it only right that all should suffer alike. Compensation was given by the Government to the sufferers, awards being made on the recommendation of a committee appointed for the purpose. It goes without saying that this unfortunate committee did not give universal satisfaction. No one for a moment supposed it would be possible to please all parties concerned. There was considerable suffering on the part of those who were exposed to the heavy rains. But the ultimate result is seen in the wider streets and the improved dwellings erected in James Town.

I had at this time the distinct advantage of attending the meetings of the Board of Education.

Not that the interests of denominational schools suffered in consequence of the absence of their respective representatives, for the very greatest consideration was given to all applications for assistance in respect of new buildings and the maintenance of school furniture and other apparatus. The Board was composed of the Governor, the members of the Legislative Council, and of such other members, not exceeding eight in number, who might be nominated by the Governor.

Grants in aid of education were made according to the results of the annual examination conducted by Her Majesty's Inspector of Schools. Attention to school management, and industry on the part of teachers and scholars were amply rewarded, for the grants were very generous. By the introduction of moderate school fees it was possible to render any school independent of missionary financial support. It is only right that it should here be stated that although the grants to Mission schools were generous, yet the education in central schools of the various missions, while equally efficient, was certainly much less costly to the Colony, than that given in purely Government schools. It will, of course, be understood that teachers in the former were willing to accept lower stipends than was the case in the latter, but uniformity, as far as the native staff was concerned, might have been effected with advantage to the Colony.

It need scarcely be said that assisted schools were

open to children without distinction of religion or race, and that no child was compelled to "attend religious instruction" when objections were made "by the parent or guardian of such child." Happily such objections were never known.

The walls of our Aburi house, forming the girls' school and dormitory, were substantially and beautifully built, before Mr. Arthur Hall left the Coast. I therefore fondly hoped that, as the framework was fitted in England, and that as doors, windows, &c., were coming out already made up, the house would be fitted together like a puzzle. But I was over sanguine—there was a pause in the proceedings, an awful pause. At intervals of three weeks, three of the Coast vessels discharged heavy cargoes for us, and when the whole consignment was collected and stored, there seemed to be enough material to build extensive barracks. The greatest "puzzle" for the time being was to get that material up the "mountain." I thought, in my innocence, that as there had been so many volunteers for labour there would be no difficulty in moving the stuff. But I was reckoning without my host. A timber waggon was secured, a gang of mountain labourers came down to fetch the first load—but they never came again. As events proved, there were a hundred loads remaining. "For de sake of going to Akla we no fit to work for you!" said the bushmen. In vain did I entreat, almost to the extent of going on my knees. I verily believed they would have almost

MISS ELLENBERGER. ABURI GIRLS' SCHOOL.

SPECIMENS OF NATIVE DRESS.

[To face page 204.

suffered starvation rather than undertake the work.
The labourers in the town were precisely of the
same mind. Not a soul would move in that direction. Days, weeks, a month passed. What with
exposure to the sun, vainly seeking help, and worry
consequent upon the information that "de white ant
was 'chopping' de wood," I had two or three days
of illness. A good-hearted native neighbour came
to pay a visit of sympathy. It should be mentioned
that visits of sympathy in West Africa are visits of
absolute silence. Yes; very much after the style of
Job's three friends, "none spake a word unto him."
It is so all along the Coast. I suppose that to the
native the sight of a number of silent friends—I do
not for one moment question the reality of their
sympathy—affords some sort of comfort, but I am
afraid that with Englishmen that kind of expression
does not help matters much. My neighbour, however, was more practical than his fellows. As he
left me he reflected thus: "For de sake of de sticks
not going to Aburi, de Reverend is sick"! The
next day he came again and generously offered to
harness his little horse for the purpose of taking a
load to a village fifteen miles on the way; further,
he dare not go, for the dreaded tsetse fly belt lay
beyond, and his horse's life would not have been
worth a pin's fee had he exceeded the distance.
After doing the journey twice he found that he had
undertaken too much, but he nevertheless gave
practical proof of his sincerity by contributing a

sum of money equal to the cost of removing ten loads.

Other friends gave advice, "Send to the Kru coast and get a gang of labourers. You will never remove your stuff until you get Kru boys; the natives are far too lazy!" But help was nearer than I anticipated. A purser of one of the passing steamers had a small gang of labourers on his hands; they had been ordered for a Cape Coast mahogany trader. No one had appeared to claim them, consequently their passages were not paid; they were in mortal fear of going down to that mysteriously comprehensive region known as "The Rivers." I might have them for the payment of their passage money and the additional half dollar per head which had been paid over to the Liberian government for the unspeakable privilege of leaving that country. I lost no time in going to the ship, and felt almost ready to embrace the "boys." What a hungry gang they looked! They were as thin—well, positively thinner, even, than their new master; and their combined wardrobes would not have realised threepence among ordinary native labourers. I felt something like a slave-owner as I paid out seventeen and sixpence per head for the nine boys. The labourers, on the other hand, felt very much like emancipation, for they had had a nightmare at the thought of going to "The Rivers." Two of them rejoiced in the very suggestive sobriquets of "Bestman" and "Trybest"; as such they, with the others, were duly registered in the stamped agreement prepared in the Commissioner's Court—a precaution observed by all employers of Kru labour —for, as my sympathetic neighbour remarked, "If you no do so, dem Kru boys humbug you too much." The agreement was to hold good for twelve months, during which time I was to pay wages at the average rate of sixteen shillings a month, plus threepence a day for "subsistence." It may here be mentioned that thousands of labourers from the Ivory and Liberian coasts annually indenture themselves in this way. Commanders of merchant vessels are dependent on Kru labour for the discharge of their cargoes, and European and native merchants are most thankful for their willing service. These men are also found, I believe, on Her Majesty's gunboats as stokers, &c. It is difficult to realise what would become of the West African trade if these labourers went out "on strike." Of all the natives on the coast the Kru boy carries the palm for lying and thieving. But his cheerfulness and comparative industry are proverbial, and I shall ever feel grateful to the memory of my gang for the care with which they carried the heaviest, as well as the most fragile articles, the long, toilsome journey to the mountain, at all hours of the day and night.

The ordinary native labourer views the Kru boy with contempt, but when the latter predominate in a given neighbourhood, they regard the native labourer as an ignoramus. "You be 'bushman!'"

said John to Mensah, "you be bushman, too much, you 'chop' kassada and koko; me no be bushman, me chop *lice* (rice)." This is regarded as abuse. "He 'buse me, sah! he 'buse me too much!" The Kru boy understands English as she is spoke in West Africa. "Now, Andrew, you see dem iron pillar, if you go drop 'em, you go broke 'em, and if you broke 'em, I fit to chop you pay one moon." The Kru boy looked askance at the new Jubilee coin when it first came out. Said he, "Dis be no Inglis money, dis (pointing to the Queen's head) be Portuguese mammy!"

On one occasion, while the roof of our new house was being fixed, I received the startling intelligence that "de house was trying to fall down!" This unlooked-for spectacle came about in consequence of our being compelled to fix the roof before attempting to furnish central supports for same, in the form of partition walls of the superstructure. The latter could not be placed in position, as we had no floor laid. The practical builder in England had said, "First fix your floor," &c.; the practical builder on the spot pointed out that days of alternate shower and sunshine would produce a sad effect upon the floor, and so it was decided to put up the roof in order to afford protection to the material below. The threatened calamity, happily, was averted without serious loss of time.

I grieve to say that, from first to last, the building operations lasted fifteen months. But there the house now stands, "beautiful for situation." Our Swiss friends have assured us that, viewed from the plain below, it suggests a mountain chalet. I trust that it may long stand, and prove a blessing to the residents, the Europeans who have the management, or who may be there for the benefit of their health, and the girls who have the advantages of education and domestic training.

CHAPTER XIII

IMPROVED LOCOMOTION IN OUR JOURNEYING—THE ARRIVAL OF MISS A. I. JACKMAN, AND HER LAMENTED DEATH—MISS MARY H. KINGSLEY—MISSIONARY METHODS AND MISSIONARY CONVERTS AND THEIR CRITICS—THE DEVOTION OF BASLE MISSIONARIES—AN ILLUSTRATION OF THE POWER OF THE GOSPEL

AFTER ten months of bachelor life, I had the joy of welcoming my wife, who was accompanied by Miss A. I. Jackman, the principal of our proposed girls' school, and the Rev. Thomas Morris, who came out to fill the vacancy created by Mr. Hall's transference to another sphere of labour.

Building operations had proved so much slower than we had anticipated, that our house was little more than half completed, and therefore the idea of taking up our residence at Aburi was postponed for a few months. The result proved disastrous and painful, as we shall see. In the meantime my good wife suggested that a brief visit to the new home was desirable, in order to arrange as to the requisite furniture. The eventful journey will ever live in our memories. Our kind neighbour, the proprietor of the pony, very considerately proposed that, in order

GRAND BASSA LABOURERS.

A HALT IN THE FOREST.   [*To face page* 210.

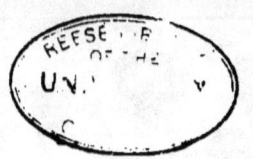

to accelerate the journey, he should drive us as far as the tsetse fly would allow him, and that the handcart with native labourers should there be in readiness to take us forward. Very naturally we gratefully consented. My good friend had, on more than one occasion, placed the service of the trap at my disposal, emphatically declaring that the horse and the cart were for me. In anticipation of my lady's arrival the high-wheeled conveyance had been most gorgeously painted, and, withal, there were two very suggestive little seats fixed near the driver. But we could boast of only one child, and even he was four thousand miles away, for no parent, with a knowledge of the country, would dream of taking a little one to that inhospitable land.

The owner considerately offered to drive, explaining that the horse knew his boy and would "humbug" him, and us. For the first two miles we went along splendidly, then the quadruped decided that he had had quite as much exercise as he cared for, and paused. There were, indeed, occasions when he was quite willing to go forward; but, unfortunately for us, the turnings that he decided to take did not lead in the direction that we wished to travel. A few miles further, and then the thoughtful owner, who was a gentleman of weight, decided that he needed a little pedal exercise: the reins and whip were accordingly handed over to me. The entertainment lasted about half an hour. I concluded that as the effect of the climate was to convert horses into mules, it was not surprising that even mankind, in that part of the world, should occasionally develop mule-like tendencies. I explained to the worthy proprietor that I was needing a little change and exercise, and accordingly dismounted. The reins and whip had no sooner changed hands than away went the fiery steed, at such a rate as to recall the exploits of Mr. John Gilpin.

The experience with the hand-cart afforded a little variety. We were descending a hill at a rapid rate; the shaft of the cart was in the hands of a man who assured us of his experience in such work, when, without a moment's warning, one wheel found its way to an embankment. Luckily I was on the side nearest to the road, so that my wife had her fall broken. Two men who had volunteered their assistance in pushing the cart, with most commendable presence of mind, fled. This experience was not quite so serious as that which befell a fellow-countryman, who was travelling at midnight, far away from any hospitable lodging, when suddenly an accident occurred, the hammock strings came asunder, giving the occupant a rude awakening, only to discover that every man had fled, he knew not where.

The shock on such occasions is usually only of a temporary character. The gentlest soul, possessed with an ordinary amount of determination, may travel at any hour of the day or night, without the slightest fear.

The first six weeks of Miss Jackman's African residence were spent at Accra. It is needless to say that the girls, attending our school, greatly appreciated the attention : they had never had such an experience. How intensely happy was the new worker, when surrounded by her little black friends! How earnestly she hoped that the senior girls would soon be teaching their fellows! What unspeakable pleasure it gave her to select for the children presents sent from England by various friends! What a treat it was to her to relate Scripture stories to the scholars attending the Sunday School! How earnestly she pleaded with the young people to live devoted Christian lives!

At Cape Coast Miss Jackman found a still wider sphere of usefulness. For here we had a much greater number of children about us. The infants reciprocated the love that was shown them. In a very short time the teacher was loved in every home that was represented in our school. But, as at Accra, six weeks was to be the limit of service at Cape Coast; at the end of that period a slight indication of fever was perceptible; in its incipient stage the attack was so slight that an old resident might have been tempted to regard the matter lightly. But we deemed it prudent to exercise the utmost care. There was much to help our friend towards speedy recovery, she was possessed of a strong constitution, of a cheerful temperament, was absolutely without fear of the dreadful climate. It need hardly be said that she had exercised the utmost care in her diet, and in her illness she was constantly attended by those who anticipated her every want. Medical aid was always near; the doctor was in constant attendance. For six days the unfailing thermometer registered only one degree of fever; then it slowly rose three degrees. A medical consultation was held, we were assured that there were no serious symptoms. Four hours later, notwithstanding the application of prescribed remedies, the thermometer registered an additional six degrees, the patient became unconscious, and died two hours later.

It has been my painful lot to witness the death of many of my fellow-countrymen in that Land of Death—more than I care to think about. The effect of the climate is to make one supremely callous about one's recovery. There naturally comes the momentary reflection, "What will they say at home?" The young man, fresh from home, thinks sorrowfully of "mother." The married man thinks of wife and home. Sometimes there is, indeed, a desperate fight for life. But usually the patient becomes indifferent. In the scene that we remember so vividly there was no indifference. There were, indeed, regrets that opportunities for usefulness were at an end, and there were loving messages for those who, it was known, would be broken-hearted when they should hear the news. The two medical attendants expressed their surprise that, with such an extraordinary temperature, there was not the faintest sign of convulsion. The last words uttered during consciousness were, "Thank you very much for all your kind attention. You have been very, very kind. For ever with the Lord!—Jesus saves me now—I see Jesus. Good bye, dear friends—Saviour!" We had but one thought, when the face of the departing soul beamed so radiantly at the sight of Him whom she had loved and served so faithfully; it was that some of our sceptical friends might have had the privilege of seeing that heavenly smile.

Miss Jackman's death was the second in a long list of six weary months of devastation. The first half of 1895 will be remembered by all who were living in that pestilential land. Closely following on the death of our friend and fellow-worker, Mrs. Kemp was prostrated by a precisely similar attack. Providentially, at the "eleventh hour"—or rather at the end of the sixth day—an old medical friend. Dr. Connolly, arrived on the scene, with new ideas respecting the treatment of fever. Drastic measures were resorted to, and the life was saved. We have special reason to be grateful to the genial surgeon, for he had had scarcely any sleep during the previous forty-eight hours, having been in constant attendance on the sick at Accra.

A voyage to Sierra Leone completed the recovery to health and strength. Fancy a voyage to Sierra Leone for the benefit of one's health It will of course be understood that emphasis is laid upon the *voyage*. Nevertheless, it may be mentioned that within recent years the health of Europeans at Free Town has been less unsatisfactory than at the Gold Coast.

While staying at Free Town we were the guests of the Reverend J. Bridge, who proved to be the very soul of kindness. We also had the pleasure of renewing our friendship with the Bishop of the diocese, at Bishop's Court, and with Canon Taylor Smith.

An altogether unlooked-for pleasure was in store for us, on our return voyage to Cape Coast. On board the *Batanga* we had the pleasure of meeting Lady Macdonald, who was on her way to Sir Claude, Consul-General for H.B.M. Niger Coast Protectorate, and Miss Mary H. Kingsley. We were assured by the commander that we might make ourselves perfectly at ease, for he had never had the pleasure of entertaining more agreeable passengers. It was further suggested that any information respecting the Coast would be of value to Miss Kingsley, inasmuch as that lady was most anxious to learn anything and everything that would be of interest concerning the manners and customs of the various peoples.

We found in Miss Kingsley exactly what the captain's description led us to expect, an unaffected inquirer, who was anxious to arrive at the truth of things. We also found that she was as opposed to all cant and snobbishness as was her distinguished uncle, Canon Kingsley. The results of Miss Kingsley's travels are well known. The substance of her remarks on missions has, in some quarters, met with adverse criticism. I suppose it will be considered natural for me to say that in her search for missionary information she was not always happy in her authorities. In the course of various conversations on the *Batanga*, I ventured to express my regret that Canon Kingsley had not a more intimate knowledge of Methodists when he wrote his novels, for I imagined that he would not, in that case, have depicted the characters he has presented to the world. I am afraid that this remark applies to Miss Kingsley, and the results of her investigation into missionary converts and missionary methods.[1] I have the less reluctance in saying this, for the reason that the writer of *Travels in West Africa* has been good enough to say the most kind things respecting the Gold Coast Mission and its workers. The favourable references to us made in the kindest possible manner are much more than we have deserved. I hope I shall not appear ungracious if I say that we

---

[1] It should be stated that towards the close of his life the Canon considerably modified his views concerning Methodists, so that we have good hope that with more personal knowledge of the subject she has so severely criticised, Miss Kingsley, with her characteristic candour, will follow the Canon's example.

entirely disclaim any right to commendation for our "noble" purposes; we undertook the work, certainly, in a moment of self-sacrifice, but anything that has savoured of heroism has long since been banished from our minds. Strange as it may appear, the real sacrifice is made in having to sever our connection with the interesting work. None the less do we gratefully acknowledge the kindly references. But we must here point out to the critic that it is the Missionaries themselves—not Exeter Hall—not the mission-loving public at home—that are largely responsible for the methods employed on the mission field. These methods are based upon the advice of Missionaries whose aggregate of experience in the service amounts to hundreds of years. And, assuming that Missionaries are not merely machines, and certainly are not compelled to exist in that climate—for every Missionary is a volunteer—we ought surely to claim for them the exercise of intelligence in the methods they employ.

Evidence respecting mission work, which is gleaned on ship-board,[1] must be taken *cum grano salis*. The friends of temperance in this country once sent out a representative to inquire into the consumption of spirits on the West Coast. The

[1] It will be observed from the study of the coast "yarns" recorded in her *Travels*, that Miss Kingsley did not accept all that was stated by the trader; but an old proverb tells us that mud thrown at an object sometimes unfortunately sticks, and I fear that the Missionary and his converts have suffered from the pelting of the trader.

information given on the ss. ——, apparently in all seriousness, was such that on "totting up" and "averaging out," we found that sufficient liquor was furnished to each customer to admit of his taking a swimming bath therein. It is earnestly hoped that the inquirer remained long enough in Africa to learn that the long bow had been drawn at a venture.

We have very pleasant recollections of voyages in various ships, and were always treated with consideration by the commanders. I remember, however, one officer who so far forgot himself as to deride the Missionary on account of the shortcomings of the "blacks." Hearing a ship's labourer make use of an oath—the import of which he certainly would not understand—the officer turned to the Missionary in the presence of the passengers, and asked if it was upon such scum as that that English money had been squandered. The inquirer evidently overlooked the fact that not all natives are Christians, just as not all Englishmen are gentlemen. He also overlooked the saddest part of the incident, viz., that the black had been taught such language by vile English lips. The fellow-passengers appreciated the reminder. The same brave officer on another occasion was having a thrust at the Missionary, when the latter turned the conversation by suggesting that during the officer's twenty-five years' experience "up and down the Coast," he must have seen a good many crocodiles. "Hundreds!" replied our hero. "Then your observation of them will enable you to tell us what is the length of a crocodile's tongue?" "Well, now, come," said the authority, "that depends upon the size of the croc'. A croc' five feet long will have a tongue one foot long. What say you——?" turning to a gentleman from the Oil Rivers. When it was suggested by the Missionary that a crocodile had no tongue he collapsed, not really knowing whether it had or had not. The probability is that he had not seen any, for they are seldom seen from the deck of a Coast steamer. The guffaw of the company gave the officer a very rosy complexion. For a time he wisely refrained from referring to himself as an authority on missions or on crocodiles. I am thankful to testify that, as far as my own experience has served, there has not been an unpleasantly close connection between crocodiles and Missionaries; nevertheless, I hope the moral contained in my anecdote will not be missed.

The critic who is much more worthy of our serious notice is the trader. But we find that there are traders *and* traders. Let us first deal with the less trustworthy representative. At the breakfast table in the saloon, for the information of the company in general, and the Missionary in particular, the loud-voiced trader declaims against missionary converts. The Missionary is sorely tempted to retaliate, "When you came on board this vessel you were in such a drunken state, and your language was so filthy that I feared you were suffering from *delirium tremens.* Who would dream of quoting you as an authority on the standard of West African morality?" But the Missionary treats him with the contempt he deserves.

The trader whose criticism we respect is the gentleman who has some regard for the feelings of those whose methods he questions. Moreover, he has lived among the natives for a dozen years. He has had them in his office, and about his home. He tells you that, notwithstanding the efforts of the Missionaries the natives are a "queer lot." He himself has been repeatedly duped by those in whom he had confidence. At the same time he very honestly admits that one reason for his not having discovered good qualities in the native is, obviously, that it has never been his particular business to look for them. All the bad qualities naturally come to the surface, and consequently are under his immediate notice. With a smile and a significant shrug he very frankly acknowledges that the influences of some of his fellows upon the morality of the native are not in every case conducive to the development of a noble character. And he also tells you that even natives of Christian England, by some mysterious means, are occasionally sent home, almost at a moment's notice.

Now the Missionary has heard the coarse criticism

emanating from the ruffian type. It is needless to say that this has no weight with him. He has also heard the criticism of those whom he respects. What has he to say in reply? First of all, that the recital of the grievances by the most considerate critic is not anything like as depressing as is his own actual experience. He is disappointed because he had fondly imagined that all who profess to be Christians are so in reality, and because he discovers that even they who are striving to live up to the light they possess have not attained to the desired standard. But notwithstanding the numberless disappointments, he will also tell you that, after making due allowance for the native and his surroundings, the disadvantages under which he is found, and the inadequate efforts that are made to uplift the race, he is prepared to state that the results of evangelistic agencies bear most favourable comparison with those put forth in England. The Missionary who has not this deep-abiding conviction must be a contemptible object, to remain in a land where his talents are wasted.

Shall we accept the suggestion of our friends and devote more time and attention to industrial education? This is a question which must be decided in detail by each worker for himself. Broadly speaking, we recognise the duty of placing within the power of our converts the means of honest self-support. And, just as social work is being more and more largely taken up by the Christian Church at home,

NATIVES OF AKWAPIM.

[*To face page* 222.

so should corresponding work be found collaterally with Mission work abroad. But we would as soon think of substituting technical education for the teaching of the Gospel, as we would think of closing the churches in this land while we go in search of the "submerged tenth."

We are thankful for good advice and kindly criticism, but at present we see no reason to alter our methods. We believe, and believe implicitly, that the Gospel of Christ is the power of God unto salvation to the savage of Africa, as well as to the highly civilised Englishman.

We have now to turn our attention to another interruption in our work. Mr. Main, who had only a short time previously returned from furlough, was laid aside with fever. In order to control the temperature, which threatened to rise rapidly, it was found necessary to bathe the patient with evaporating lotions. On one occasion I took charge of the process for five hours, without a pause, for the thermometer had registered 106°. As soon as convalescence was assured, a voyage to Grand Canary was advised. Fortunately for us our good friend and neighbour, Mr. Batty, was a passenger to England in the same vessel, so that our colleague was in good hands. Six weeks later Mr. Main was back again, and within a few days was again prostrated by a still more persistent attack. Once again he cheated the King of Terrors, but looked such a wreck that when taken to the ship for England, the surgeon, mistaking Mr. Somerville for the medical attendant, inquired if the patient was brought aboard so as to die at sea—a precaution, by the way, which it is said thoughtful Spanish physicians at Grand Canary take, in order that the mortality at their fair island may not be affected.

For a fortnight the patient lay between life and death; notwithstanding the assiduous attention of the ship's surgeon and Dr. Cross of the Niger. As a matter of fact the local newspaper reported the death as having occurred near Sierra Leone. The last week of the voyage worked such wonders that Mr. Main found it necessary to explain in England that he had really been ill.

One wearies of recording these instances of sickness, for it must be a tax on the reader's patience. But what the actual experience is none but the resident can realise. It is of the greatest importance that all who have interests in any form in West Africa should know that the best devised plans in the hands of those who are worthy of confidence are constantly in danger of being disturbed.

Commercial interests at the Gold Coast are represented by so many hundreds of thousands of pounds. The Missionary Society's interests cannot be thus estimated, but they are not, on that account, of less importance. We had hoped that Mr. Somerville would have been enabled to pay lengthened visits to all our schools in the district, and thus have rendered the valuable aid he had been enabled to give at Cape Coast, but the breakdown referred to above upset all our arrangements.

The greater part of 1895 was spent at Aburi, when we were enabled to complete our building arrangements, and provide a home for the convalescent from the Missionary, the Government and the Merchant Services. We had the pleasure of welcoming the Rev. J. S. Ellenberger in the place of Mr. Main. The new Missionary rendered invaluable help with the somewhat complicated accounts of the district. Our pleasure was very great when, a few months later, he was joined by his sister. Their devotion to the work has been such that, notwithstanding repeated protestations, they have denied themselves the common necessaries of life in order that from their own funds they might supplement the local resources. We had also the pleasure of a more intimate acquaintance with our friends of the Basle Missionary Society.

I have elsewhere shown that, as a Mission, our own Society has been far behind the Lutheran Society in some respects. I must take this opportunity of bearing testimony to the self-sacrificing devotion of its representatives. It is customary when speaking of the devotion of Missionaries to regard the agents of the Roman Catholic Church as being the very embodiment of self-sacrifice. As I write, a friend sends me the *National Review* for December, 1897, wherein I find "A Cross-bench

View of Foreign Missions"; written, presumably, by an Anglican clergyman. I cull therefrom a sentence, "A passionate missionary ardour has marked the history of Vaticanism." Another sentence runs thus, "Nowhere does the Roman Church wear so noble and Christian an aspect as in the Mission field." I yield to no one in my admiration of the devoted nuns of the Lyons Mission at the Gold Coast. No one can have witnessed their lives without being struck with their self-denial. But I must personally say that I never met with such sacrifice as was exemplified in the life of a Lutheran minister whom I met at Aburi. He had heard of our intention of leaving the Coast early the following year, and therefore came to ask if we would undertake the care of his two youngest children as far as London, and he would arrange for them to be met by a friend from Germany. Of course we consented. But I asked, "Why not wait until you go yourself? You can care for them so much better than we can." He replied, with tears in his eyes, "The children need a change; they ought to go soon. I do not like to keep them. And besides, I would rather spare the two now than have to spare them when next I return from furlough; for then I shall have to say 'good-bye' to five children besides, and the trial would be too great!" Those of my readers who have children of their own will understand that every sacrifice that the Missionary may make sinks into utter insignificance compared with the sacrifice

HOTEL ACCOMMODATION.

[To face page 226.

of the children of one's own flesh and blood. I admired this self-sacrifice the more for the reason that I knew so well that my friend had experienced a good deal of disappointment in his work. And that if any man had cause to say that the natives were ungrateful and unworthy of the kindness shown them, he certainly had greater cause.

The Rev. J. Müller, of Akropong, who had been in the Colony, I believe, nearly forty years, I learned to esteem and love. It was always a great pleasure to meet with the Rev. and Mrs. Groh and Dr. and Mrs. Fisch. The Doctor was most kind in his professional attendance, and his experience and counsel as a Missionary were invaluable. I remember his once remarking that if the worker was anxious to be discouraged he might easily attain the desired end. He might compare one week's work with another to find that no progress had been made; or he might point to a number of professed Christians whose lives would justify the onslaught of the hypercritic. "But that," said he, "is scarcely the fair view of the matter. You have to make comparisons between tens or twenties of years' work."

About the time of which I write an opportunity was afforded me of reminding the natives of Aburi of the influence of the Gospel upon the masses of those who had embraced its teaching. The occasion was the celebration of the anniversary of the Basle Mission Church. Most gladly accepting the invitation to give an address at the meeting, I ventured to draw a picture of the condition of the country at the time that the Gospel was first introduced there. I ought to say that the audience numbered, as far as I can remember, about five hundred, including a band of some thirty or forty young men who were being educated and trained as catechists, school teachers, and pastors to their fellow-countrymen. In the course of my address I mentioned that only a few hours previously I had received by post half a dozen magazines, fifty years old. My mother had sent them to me knowing that, as they contained references to the Gold Coast and Ashanti Mission, they would be of special interest to me. One of the numbers furnished an account of a human sacrifice that was offered. The victim selected was a woman with a babe at her breast. The Missionary no sooner heard the report than he hastened to the scene of execution in order to save, at least, the child. He found the body of the woman. The head was struck off, and had rolled away at a little distance, and the wretched babe was licking the blood as it flowed from the corpse. The Missionary ran forward to take the child. The executioner understood the motive, and in an instant he placed his foot on the neck of the child and crushed out its life. I might, with perfect truth, have said to my audience, "And such were some of you, but ye are washed, ye are sanctified, ye are justified in the name of the Lord Jesus, and by the spirit of our God." At the period that the above horrible incident was first recorded, the streets of Aburi at times ran with human blood. (I gratefully recognise the important part which the British Government has taken in the suppression of horrible customs in West Africa, and shall attempt, in the next chapter, to pay a respectful tribute.) "A really converted African is a very beautiful form of Christian," writes Miss Kingsley. A really converted African, who, after all, is a "missionary made man," as far as human agency is concerned, is a striking contrast to the man who hacked his fellows before he became a convert. As I looked round upon my audience and noted the reverence, I thought, "Well, even if these men and women are not on an equality with the highly favoured peoples of Europe, they certainly have made an advance since the Gospel was first proclaimed among them." The contrast between their former condition and the state in which I then beheld them, reminded me of a picture which is presented to the readers of the New Testament in the fifth chapter of the Gospel of St. Mark.

CHAPTER XIV

THE BRITISH OCCUPATION OF ASHANTI—A RESPECTFUL TRIBUTE TO THE BRITISH ARMY AND NAVY AS AGENTS THAT MAKE FOR JUSTICE AND MERCY—AN ACCOUNT OF A JOURNEY TO KUMASI

AMONG the many luxuries we enjoyed at the Gold Coast was the receipt of a weekly cablegram from Reuter. This privilege cost the subscribers a guinea a year. The Government of the Colony contributed very generously towards the total cost. Although we were in the "bush" of Aburi, we felt we were not so far from home when we could receive, a few hours after its despatch from London, a cablegram as follows:—"British ultimatum. Venezuela demands reparation. Salisbury Warden Cinque Ports. First-class battleship *Victorious* launched."

On October 21st the cable read: "Scott arrived; interviewed by Reuter's agent at Liverpool Urged occupying Coomassie; numerous offers from special officers to serve in Ashanti campaign. Armenian reforms granted." So Sir Francis had urged the occupation of Ashanti. Every disinterested native of the Gold Coast, as well as every European, felt that there was no other course open to the General.

I have introduced the qualifying word "disinterested." It is just possible that there were a handful of natives whose sympathies were with the monarch of Ashanti; but, generally speaking, it was felt that further delay in carrying out much-needed reforms in Ashanti would be inconsistent with common humanity.

I do not know that I altogether blame the savages of Ashanti for their awful practices, "*for they did it ignorantly and in unbelief.*" I hesitate, however, to say as much concerning the policy of the princes in insisting on proceeding to England in spite of the repeated warnings of Sir Brandford Griffith—I am afraid that they were either lacking in intelligence or in principle in diametrically opposing that Governor's instructions. What humiliation they might have spared themselves, what disappointment and mortification their monarch if they had only returned to Kumasi and declared emphatically that the British Government insisted on carrying out reforms in the country; and that, as a tangible proof of the monarch's willingness to acquiesce, it was required that a British resident should be received in the capital. Instead of acting like wise men the princes puffed themselves up with the idea that they would be received at the Colonial Office if not at the British Court, thus it came about that an expensive mission to England was arranged: the sequel is too well known to need repetition. I am not altogether prepared to blame that section of the British public which was so completely gulled by the statements of the princes, for I imagine that a mysterious spell was cast over them and they were helpless. But it would have been an awful calamity to have ignored Her Majesty's Representative in the Colony. There are natives in Africa who have yet to learn that, so long as the Representative of the Government, or of the Commercial House, or of the Missionary Society, has the confidence of those whom he represents, his authority must be recognised—the only alternative must be to recall the Representative. Sir Brandford Griffith, through whom the negotiations, which ultimately led to the fitting out of the expedition, were conducted, was the very soul of considerateness, as far as the aborigines were concerned. He seemed to be possessed of the patience of Job when conducting their affairs.

Although not necessarily avowed Christian men in every instance, yet the officers of the two services serving under Her Majesty's flag represent Justice and Humanity. Ancient history furnishes illustrations of the manner in which it pleased God to make use of heathen Governments for the purpose of accomplishing His plans. Some of my readers who hold pronounced peace-at-any-price views, may pityingly smile at the parson's justification of the sword; but I should consider myself worse than despicable if I failed to declare my firm conviction that the British Army and Navy are to-day used by

[To face page 232.

AKIM EXECUTIONER.   KING'S STOOL CARRIER.

God for the accomplishment of His purposes. I was once looking at the portrait of a naval officer when a friend remarked: "That's a portrait of an uncle of mine who was in command of a gunboat in the South Seas. He was not a decided Christian, but on one occasion he gave a passage in his vessel to two Missionaries from one island to another. While on the way he unsuccessfully tried to convince these men that they were a pair of fools for dreaming of doing any good among cannibals. But when he reached the desired port he sent for the cannibal chief, and said, "I have brought two friends of mine who want to stay in your town, and I have sent for you because I wish you to know that I hold you responsible for their safety. I am coming back again shortly, and if my friends are not forthcoming I will show you what I will do with you!" He then gave directions for a number of targets to be floated, and upon those he ordered his guns to be fired. "Now," said he, "you know exactly what to expect if you do not take care of these friends." I unhesitatingly declare my belief that these means were used by God for the preservation of the Missionaries from the cannibal cooking pots. I am, of course, well aware that the combined fleets of the world riding at anchor at Fiji would not have accomplished what the Gospel of Christ has done in that part of the world.

I hate war with all my soul; but I cannot describe the thankfulness I felt as I saw the troops disembark at Cape Coast Castle during the Christmas of 1895, for we were thus assured that brighter days were in store for the notoriously blood-stained capital of Ashanti.

Our commodious house at Cape Coast, to which reference is elsewhere made, was placed at the disposal of the late Governor, Sir W. E. Maxwell, for the use of officers, and very great pleasure we found in ministering in the slightest degree to their comfort. We were favoured on one occasion with the company of no fewer than thirty officers in the house, and as many non-commissioned officers and men in the school-room. These came to us in the middle of the month to make arrangements for the transport of the West Yorkshire Regiment and the composite battalion to Kumasi. May I add that Sir Francis Scott was good enough to introduce me to H.R.H. Prince Christian Victor, for I very much wish to say how exceedingly agreeable the Prince was to his fellow-countrymen—how anxious that he should be regarded as an ordinary officer, prepared to rough it with the rest of his comrades.

It need scarcely be said that some of the young officers had previously seen no foreign service, nor had they taken lessons in the pidgin-English of the Coast. This was evident from the question addressed to a servant at 5 o'clock a.m. : "Jack, have you had your food?" I see Jack's blank look now. The question needed interpretation—"Jack, you get you chop?" "No, sah!" Had my friend known his man he might have understood that Jack would have looked after "Number One;" but it is not usual to take "breffus" until the middle of the day.

It had been arranged by our Army and Navy Committee with the War Office, that I should accompany the troops to Kumasi, but my colleague Somerville was most desperately anxious to go to the front; and as our house partook more or less of the character of an hotel, and consequently needed a proprietor, I made arrangements for Mr. Somerville to be attached to the West Yorkshire Regiment. But, although the ordinary missionary work was for a time suspended, there were other duties requiring attention. The hospital at the "base of operations" received a great number of patients, and these came under my charge; while the Nonconformists connected with the West African squadron also received such attention as we were able to give.

I was honoured with an invitation to conduct divine service on H.M.S. *Racoon*. The captain took the precaution to assure himself that there was not the slightest difference between my theology and that of the Anglican Church—as taught, say, by the Church Missionaries. I was in a position to give the assurance; for, until I reached early manhood I was a member of the ancient Church. No small amount of assurance was needed to stand before the ship's company on that particular morning, for it happened that the most prominent feature of my face was disfigured by an excruciatingly painful malarial protuberance, which naturally affected the risibility of Jack Tar.

A propos of oneness in regard to Scripture doctrine, I may just mention that, at the suggestion of our genial and brotherly friend, Canon Taylor Smith, the "voluntary" service on Sunday, in Kumasi, was conducted conjointly by the Canon and Somerville, and was very greatly appreciated by all who attended it. The Canon had expressed a desire that the parade service should be united, but objection was taken by one of the officers, who asked of what advantage were two chaplains if only one service was needed. A curious question for an officer to ask, in the presence of representatives of a score of different regiments, who, on that particular occasion, had joined forces for the accomplishment of our purpose, which, happily, was consummated!

"The Committee and our supporters generally are delighted with your prompt action in reference to the re-occupation of Kumasi. I trust we shall now be able to prosecute the work vigorously on our old Mission field in that country. When you have been up yourself and seen what is necessary, you must communicate with me as to financial needs, and you may be sure I shall do my best to secure the necessary funds." Such was the message communicated by our secretary, the Rev. Marshall

PREPARING TO START.

A FANTI BUSH VILLAGE.

To face page 236.

Hartley. An account of the journey to Kumasi will possibly be of interest.

At the outset I have a confession to make. I did not take with me that almost indispensable companion—the camera. My own was carefully locked up at Aburi. The photographs which I have secured will answer the purpose to illustrate the journey.

Mr. Somerville was arranging for a lengthened stay in Ashanti, and he also proposed erecting houses and schools. Hence it became necessary to take with us packages of tools; our carriers were, therefore, somewhat numerous. But when it was generally known that we wanted carriers, there was no lack of applications for employment. There is an unwritten law to the effect that journeys of more than ten miles necessitate an alternate set of hammock-men. These carriers, therefore, have a decided advantage over the ordinary carriers, whose recognised load is half a hundred-weight, but have no relief, and are, moreover, unable to induce their loads to walk up the hills. Germans have a distinctly economical mode of travelling; they simply pay the carriers for the time they are actually *in* the hammock. Viewed from the native standpoint this arrangement is hardly satisfactory, for when I once proposed adopting the method, one of our native ministers, with a serio-comic expression, exclaimed, " Heaven forbid that my lord should do so!" On making a start our compound was crowded with men, women, youths, and maidens desirous of obtaining employment. Disappointment was writ large upon the faces of those whose offers we were compelled to decline. Our faithful carpenter had proffered his services as builder-in-chief at Kumasi. We marvelled greatly at this; but we soon discovered that he wished to be "saved from his friends"; who, regarding him as the head of the family, were frequently insisting on his becoming their surety; with the result that the unfortunate man was always in debt, or answering for his "friends'" shortcomings in the Commissioner's Court. Even while taking leave of his friends he was served with a summons, which, with our assistance, was settled out of court. Carpenter Kobina Aitua had, in his earlier days, been a polygamist, but a few years since sent two of his wives away, retaining the third, for the reason that "she no humbug him too much." It is altogether impossible to say how many funerals he had attended during his stay with me. The number of his departed "brudders" was legion. I remember on one occasion he returned from paying this last tribute of respect, with sundry pieces of sticking plaster in the region of his eyes. On inquiry I learnt that a former wife had had a dispute with him at the cemetery, and had used her fingers in support of her arguments. Like most human beings Aitua has his peculiarities, but he has served us well in our workshops at Cape Coast, and, as a workman, compares very favourably with the average British joiner.

The distance from Cape Coast to Kumasi is 142 miles. Travelling on the best parts of the road was at the rate of three miles an hour, but through the narrow and rough road beyond Prahsu we slowed down to two miles an hour. The average day's journey was eighteen miles. The night's resting-places were at Dunkwa, Mansu, Fesu, Prahsu, Fumsu, Kwisa, Bekwai, Kumasi. As a general rule the day's march begins quite early, and ten or twelve miles are covered before a halt is made for a substantial breakfast, leaving the shorter portion of the journey for the afternoon. At Ekroful, near our chapel, we saw the grave of an officer who was killed during the Ashanti war. Although twenty-two years have passed away, the memory of Lieut. Mundy is still dear to his friends at home. To an African death has not the dread that it has for white races. At one of the villages we halted near an undertaker's shed, where there was a rather elaborate coffin. In answer to inquiries we were informed that the "dead man *live* for dem place (pointing away from the village); he no be dead yet!" In other words, the coffin was in readiness waiting for the last gasp of its future occupant. I have, on more than one occasion, been appealed to for the advance of a few shillings, or the loan of a few nails wherewith to prepare a coffin for one whose death was anticipated. This reminds one of the fact that an English barrister—the author of the *Land of Death*—found on recovering from a serious illness that a coffin had been prepared for him, and had actually been carried into the house. The makers thereof were greatly disgusted when they discovered that the convalescent declined to settle their account.

After leaving Mansu, we observed that over a great part of the distance the telegraph wire took a new route. As we toiled along the two sides of the triangular route, or wearily described circles, we fervently hoped that the Road Department of the Colony would, in making a new road, avail itself of the direct route so admirably marked out by the Telegraph Department. The overhanging branches of the giant cotton trees had wrought great havoc with the temporary wire. The mischief thus done suggested the enormous amount of labour and expense that would be involved in order to secure uninterrupted communication with the interior. In many instances it was evident that the monsters of the forest depend more or less—like jerry-built houses—upon one another for support. And when, as in road-making, the supports are cut away, it is seen that the appearance of strength in these trees is most deceptive. The task of removing trees and undergrowth seemed well-nigh hopeless.

On the morning of the fifth day's march, at Prahsu we were somewhat surprised at the request of the carriers to grant them a day's rest. Various reasons were suggested for the halt, such as lameness and weariness. When, however, it was known that no pay would be forthcoming, our men, with the exception of four or five Fantis and a nondescript who were anxious to remain in our employment in Kumasi, resolved to strike. It was fortunate that the men were not all of one tribe. The threat did not have the much-desired effect, and when they found that my colleague and I were prepared to walk, if necessary, they immediately changed their minds, and even the professedly lame insisted on keeping up with the company, while the weary ones suddenly became agile; we had no further trouble with any of the men. The inexperienced traveller is entirely at the mercy of the native, who certainly does not love work for its own sake. It sometimes happens that every advantage will be taken of the unfortunate victim of circumstances. The greatest firmness as well as the greatest kindness is necessary in dealing with a company of carriers. A mile to the north of Prahsu we found that the effect of the early wet season was making itself felt. For about two hundred yards the apology for a roadway was covered to a depth of eighteen inches. But the broad back of the faithful Aitua was voluntarily placed at my disposal, so that there was no delay.

At Fumsu we halted for the night. We had experienced a little difficulty on the way in procuring a light. Our cook informed us by way of explanation, that "de matches catch de cold." Our prospects certainly were not very cheering. In the centre of the courtyard was the customary fire, and upon the fire was placed the most disgustingly filthy-looking flesh, for which the natives seem to have so keen a relish. The compounds of the Adansis and Ashantis are, for the most part, about twelve feet square, and on either side are rooms about eight feet by four feet, some of them considerably narrower. The floors of these are raised about fifteen inches above the level of the court, and are plastered with a red clayey substance, which clings to nothing so tenaciously as to one's shoes and clothing. The side of the room facing the courtyard has no wall, so that windows are unnecessary; it is, of course, a difficult matter to disrobe in the strictest privacy. This is perhaps the most serious difficulty. Fortunately the rains in this part of the world generally oblige by descending in one particular direction, and the architect, who is a keen observer of the wind, takes advantage of this peculiarity, so that the bed-chamber is fairly dry at all times. The walls of the huts are constructed of a double row of sticks, placed about three inches apart, but strongly laced into position with fibre, and the whole is filled up and plastered with clay, which is to be found close at hand. Doors an inch and a half thick, and four feet six by two feet—which certainly are not convenient dimensions for lengthy or corpulent travellers—are cut from a log in one slab, and are trimmed into shape with the

HILLSIDE SCENERY.

[To face page 242.

AN EMANCIPATED SLAVE.

assistance of an adze. The roofs of the buildings are, in the first instance, substantially thatched. Residences of kings and chiefs are much more imposing —the doorways are about four feet wide, and from ten to twelve feet in height.

The least comfortable night during the whole journey was spent at Fumsu. We had both mosquitoes and sand-flies vying with each other in their attention to us. Now the most good-tempered Kru boy, who withal is inured to every hardship, will protest against such assiduous attentions. " Dem mosquito go chop we all de day; dem mosquito small brudder go chop we all de night." To add to our discomfort the rattling of the heavenly artillery was accompanied by a heavy downpour of rain which found its way through our roof. But when the morning broke with the glorious sunlight our spirits were as light as were those of the parrot's, whistling strong and free over our heads.

The ascent of the Moinsie Hills was an item in the day's programme, and we considered it prudent, after travelling ten miles, to fortify the inner man. Native food was scarce, the wretched-looking fowls, whose feathers suggest the quills on " fretful porcupine," had almost entirely disappeared. Eggs were a fabulous price, and the tough, leathery mutton and goat's flesh could not be obtained. Happily we were furnished with an English (or American) ham, which, in the most plentiful days of native food supply, is the cheapest meal procurable. But—to continue the journey.

Reports had reached us that, in order to ascend the hill, one ought to be prepared to "hang on by one's eyebrows!" We found it much less serious than we had anticipated. I did not, however, feel disposed to follow the example of my energetic companion and take the original path, but availed myself of the modern zig-zag road, which certainly possessed advantages.

We were greatly surprised on reaching Kwisa to find an enormous stock of surplus provisions, left by the expedition. Some thousands of cases of biscuits, corned beef, army rations, milk, &c., were under the charge of Captain (now Major) Donovan, A. S. C. A very considerable quantity had already been disposed of to the natives, as well as to the officers at Kumasi. The sight of the store reminded us of the perfect arrangements made by the Army Service Corps for the comfort of the troops. It was quite beyond all human knowledge to estimate the needs of the expedition. The campaign doubtless was costly, but the imposing sight of British soldiers well equipped had a salutary effect upon the Ashanti princes and chiefs as they passed through the lines, and taught them that resistance would be folly on their part.

Captain Donovan received us most hospitably. I trust that our company was welcome to this solitary officer, so far removed from his fellow-countrymen. The hut placed at our disposal was that which the lamented Prince Henry of Battenberg occupied in the early part of his fatal illness.

On the 13th March we passed Fomena, where the treaty of 1874 was signed, and Amoaful, which was the scene of one of the most serious engagements of that time. These once important places are marked on the map as "ruins," but no ruins are to be seen; the materials of former ruins have long since decayed and amalgamated with the earth. The only marks by which the places are recognised are simply the clearing of forest trees and undergrowth, now covered by grass ten feet high. We had contemplated turning aside from Dompoasi to visit Dadiasi—one of our old Mission stations. The first-named town had declined in importance owing to the unsettled state of the country. The latter was entirely depopulated in consequence of the raids of the Ashantis. How devoutly thankful we felt once again that the caprice of these tyrants could no longer be gratified.

Bekwai, another old Mission station, was reached at four o'clock. One of our native ministers had been received by the townspeople some four weeks earlier. He had, indeed, opened a school. After a very brief delay we were accommodated with lodgings. I afterwards learnt that the king makes no trouble in finding rooms for his visitors. He simply sends a message to a subject saying that his premises are wanted for a few days, and, without any demur, the owner immediately vacates them. The interval between our arrival in the town and our occupation of the rooms was about twenty minutes: ample time for the owner to arrange for and effect the transfer of every stick of furniture and all other accessories. I hinted to Mr. Baiden that this was a rather unceremonious way of dealing with subjects. He, however, seemed to think that the request was most modest. The king of Kumasi would go much further than that. At a great gathering of his subjects he would catch the eye of one of them, and ask him to oblige by having his head removed. The only condition asked by the obliging subject would be a plentiful supply of rum.

We had not been many minutes in our lodgings when our faithful henchman drew our attention to a long procession of carriers heavily laden with gifts of vegetables, &c., from the king. We inquired the cause thereof. The reply was, "Dey tink plenty soldiers come!" and truly the supply was plentiful. Our carriers were enabled to hoard up their "'sistence" money for a day or two. I ought to add that the entrance to our courtyard was protected by a fetish charm. Ought I to confess that I annexed the latter? I soothed my conscience with the reflection that its intrinsic value was considerably less than that of the horse-shoe which guards the entrances to so many English homes, and if this does not satisfy the reader, I will just add that the act of annexation did not for one moment mar the perfect good-will existing between the excellent proprietor of the establishment and ourselves. In return for an insignificant quantity of salt we were presented with a rather handsome Ashanti pipe.

The next morning we visited the king. It may here be stated that, generally speaking, His Majesty is very popular with British officers, and he certainly is most thankful to be recognised as a subject of Her Majesty. I think I may safely say that the peacefulness of the expedition depended, in a measure, upon Bekwai. The notorious fighting king of Mampon had strongly urged Prempeh to go into the field against the British forces. Prempeh felt that he could not be independent of Bekwai, and therefore sent to its king to encounter our troops near the river Prah. But to this arrangement our friendly king objected; far from opposing, he claimed the protection of the British, and in this way a more or less serious engagement was averted.

His Majesty of Bekwai does not profess to be a paragon of virtue. His harem is said to contain twenty wives—not quite so great a number as might have been expected. It is, I think, beyond question that he imbibes more spirituous liquor than is good for his constitution. But then to be a polygamist and to indulge freely in the loving-cup are the essential qualifications of an African king—at least judging from a pagan point of view. Certainly His Majesty has not the bloodthirsty traits that marked the conduct of his predecessor. During the few years that he has occupied the stool only one execution has been performed, and that was for a criminal offence. I had the information from a very reliable source that on one occasion Prempeh sent a request to Bekwai for a victim for sacrifice, but the king declined, preferring to send a present of £8 wherewith to appease the appetite of the monster.

The king received us in semi-state under his huge umbrella. He was attended by his chiefs. On his left hand was stationed a lad with a huge bunch of keys, the rusty appearance of which suggested that they were seldom used, except to denote the importance of the owner. A lad on the right of the king was deputed to rid his royal master of the flies which certainly are no respecter of persons, and are particularly objectionable in that part of the country. The chiefs and headmen took up their position on one side of the Court, the linguist, heralds and court-criers sat on the opposite side. Speaking through the linguist the king informed us that he had the most sincere regard for our old native minister, Mr. Jones, who had been in the country some years previously, but had been obliged to leave on account of the unsettled state of affairs brought about by tribal wars. He renewed his assurances of love for our work. He had already made over to us a piece of land, and would by other means encourage the Missionaries in their efforts to re-

ASHANTI GOLD WEIGHTS.

A GOLD COAST CHIEF AND VISITORS.

[*To face page* 248.

establish the work. During the delivery of the king's speech the heralds from time to time uttered exclamations which signified that their master had well spoken. The court-criers, whose distinctive badge of office was the skin of a monkey's head, meantime securing silence in Court. The visit was returned in the afternoon, when the king promised to send to our committee a small present as a slight acknowledgment of our endeavours to benefit his people. The promised token of friendship takes the form of a beautifully carved native stool, which may be seen in the Museum of our London Mission-house. I sincerely regret to have to say that the manner in which other promises have been fulfilled reminds us once again that one must be prepared to allow very generous discount in dealing with African princes.

The early service on Sunday was well attended by the aristocracy of Bekwai. The singing was wretchedly feeble, and none of the natives joined us in the Lord's Prayer. These facts alone indicate to the West African Missionary how novel such a service was to the company. Mr. Baiden informed us that the king and the queen-mother had been regular attendants at the services, which were begun in February. We have great hopes that the work will be successful in that benighted neighbourhood.

On the 16th we journeyed through Amoaful to Abodom, which we reached at nine o'clock. Here we found that a commodious bamboo building, to serve the purpose of schoolroom and chapel, was in course of erection by voluntary workers. The king was away at his farm, but returned at the request of the chiefs to welcome us. Other individuals of more or less importance responded to the call-drum. The little lad of fourteen years is the youngest king I have met. We quite fell in love with his artlessness. I sincerely trust that he will reap the benefits of education, and that it may be said of him "while he was yet young he began to seek after God."

On going to the king's house to discuss the object of our mission, we observed that the Union Jack had been unfurled in honour of our visit. It was evident that the boy-king was a mere figure-head; we were given to understand that our remarks should be addressed to the linguist. The chief, in response, without consulting the occupant of the stool, spoke through the linguist to us. Nevertheless, there was one order given by His Majesty— and that, withal, a most welcome one. We hinted that fowls were very scarce in the country. He at once issued instructions that any which might be caught in the public thoroughfare were ours, leaving it to our judgment and honesty as to payment. It was truly a wondrous spectacle to see sober elderly chiefs in hot pursuit of the feathered bipeds.

Retracing our steps to Amoaful, where we breakfasted, we were soon on the main road again. Sheltering from a heavy downpour of rain in an elaborate Fetish house at Esumeja, we travelled to

Edunku, where, for the thousand-and-first time, I dissected a West African fowl for our dinner, and we retired for the night.

Early next morning we were on the march, reaching Kumasi at 11.20. We soon derived an advantage from the Military Telegraph Department, for a telegram from my wife awaited us. We called on the Resident, Colonel Pigott, D.S.O., who received us very kindly, and invited us to a tempting breakfast. Shortly afterwards our old friend Dr. Macarthy, the Cantonment Magistrate, took us over the Royal Palace, which is now used as a prison. Here we saw the chief executioner and an assistant. The former appeared to be about the age of "threescore years and ten." The poor wretch was dreamily awaiting his fate—prepared, if necessary, to be despatched to his long home. He considered himself of small importance as an executioner; for although, according to his own confession, he had slain some thousands of victims, his work sank into utter insignificance when compared with the deeds of his predecessor. The assistant possessed a face which indicated special fitness for his bloody work. To those who hold the theory that every individual in the world resembles one or another of the lower animals, it may be of interest to say that this man's face appeared to resemble that of the tiger. I saw a knife with which executions had been performed: it was of English manufacture. The edge was very much jagged, which, it was explained, was due to the troublesome bones in the necks of the unfortunate victims.

The palace certainly has been of considerable importance in its time. Native art has excelled in rendering it quite imposing. I felt truly sorry for the officers of the expedition as they expressed their disappointment and disgust at the sorry-looking spectacle of the palace. Many of them had visited India, consequently their expectations of palatial residences ran high. Prempeh's palace is now used partly as a prison, and partly as a rest house for travellers. Two or three little rooms were pointed out to us as intended prisons for Europeans. We know that Europeans have been imprisoned in Kumasi, and we understand to a small extent how brutally they were treated, but the idea of taking English soldiers as prisoners during war certainly was too preposterous to be seriously entertained.

We were very thankful to observe that preparations were being made to ensure permanent peace. The erection of a substantial fort, capable of accommodating British officers and native soldiers together with stores of ammunition, will prove of service not only to the inhabitants of the town, but to the surrounding tribes. A space of 200 yards' radius from the fort is to be kept open. The property given to our Mission sixty years ago unfortunately comes within this area, but arrangements were made to transfer to us another site, of which more hereafter. We were just leaving the fort, when we were informed that a native labourer had fallen down the well which was being sunk to the depth of sixty feet. We anxiously waited to know the worst. We found that, although the poor fellow was unconscious and was badly bruised and bleeding, there were decided hopes of his recovery which were realised the next day. His substantial skull had saved him.

An opportunity was given us of witnessing a murder trial. Colonel Pigott was President of the Court, but, in dispensing justice, he was assisted by local chiefs. The Government has very wisely arranged to allow chiefs to have a voice in the management of local affairs, and still more wisely arranged that the decisions in court may at any time be overruled by the Resident. Were it not so ordered, judgment would invariably be entered in favour of those who could pay the most handsomely for it. A benevolent-looking linguist acted as spokesman for the chiefs. The prisoner brought into court was charged with having shot a neighbour. It was almost a foregone conclusion that the accused was guilty. But the evidence of the afternoon was decidedly in his favour. Witnesses proved that the prisoner and the deceased had always lived on the most friendly terms. Furthermore, the prisoner was able, by firing in a similar manner at a board placed at a corresponding distance, to support his defence that he mistook the deceased for an animal in the long grass. The poor wretch excited our deepest pity. Evidently he was more bewildered by the surroundings than by the awfulness of the charge preferred against him. How nervously he fumbled the clumsy flint-lock gun while reloading it! He seemed to be at least fifteen minutes in completing his arrangements. We could not but reflect that any British officer with a spark of manliness must have felt devoutly thankful that events were so ordered as to spare him the necessity of wholesale butchery of these savages by Maxim guns.

The President was greatly perplexed by the relationships of witnesses to one another, and to the accused. It occurred to us that the Colonel had yet to learn that the solitary son of African parents may have a dozen or a score of "brudders." "Not de same fadder, and not de same mudder!" The custom of the country is to schedule all sterner relatives in the paternal and fraternal columns. Fellow-workmen and co-religionists are similarly classified. The gentler relatives and acquaintances are known as mothers and sisters.

I ascertained that the Government has consented to allow the execution of criminals to be carried out after the custom of the country, safeguarding such executions from cruelty by appointing a surgeon to be present. The execution of criminals in Ashanti has, I believe, always differed from the mode of executing victims in sacrifice. In the former case the hands of the criminal were fixed behind his back, and the executioner, making a leopard-like spring upon the criminal, would " hack " the neck in a manner too horribly revolting to be described. In the case of sacrifice it would be by means of a heavier knife; the victim was prevented from cursing the executioners (for such a curse was greatly dreaded) by means of an iron skewer passed through the cheeks and tongue! He was then required to kneel, with his head over a huge bath. I hesitate to write these words. But I feel that it is a responsibility to know that "the dark places of the earth are full of the habitations of cruelty." We remonstrate with the chiefs of Kumasi. Their retort is: " Your ancestors were savages, and did the same!" But we have to reply, " Not to that awful extent; and even supposing they did, is that any reason why you should be allowed to continue such brutal practices?"

I have in my possession a skull, obtained from the " Golgotha" of Kumasi, concerning which a medical friend writes:—" Notwithstanding its prognathous character (this is not so well seen, as the lower jaw is absent) there is a fair development of brain, and, though thicker than a European skull, it is not so thick as that of an aboriginal Australian. The large dint on one side is due to some injury during birth or the first year of life. The roughness at the hinder part of the vertex is due to long and severe ulceration, brought about by dirt and the manner of dressing the hair. The skull is probably between thirty and forty years old. The condition of the jaw shows that the victim had had rather hard times in the way of hard food, and suffered in consequence. A small process was cut off the skull in decapitation; other portions from each side of the face were removed subsequently. The vault of the skull suggests that there was not much intellect."

A native minister, who has seen numbers of headless victims, tells me that the greatest barbarity was practised on murderers. During the greater part of the day appointed for the execution the criminal would be led with hands secured behind him through the streets of the town, the crowd meanwhile insulting and scoffing. Towards evening one of the executioners would ironically ask the prisoner to carry the knife, as he himself was tired. This request was instantly followed by the brute burying the knife in the flesh at the shoulder-bone. Other executioners would follow this example, taking care that no vital part of the body was wounded —an error which would have speedily terminated his sufferings.

The journey had more than ever impressed me with the fact that the expedition was a most righteous one. The whole journey beyond Prahsu furnished endless proof that the British Government was more than justified in protecting those who had so long been under the sway of the misguided chiefs of Kumasi. On the other hand, it must be admitted that Ashanti but furnishes an illustration of the spirit

KING PREMPEH AND SUITE AT ELMINA CASTLE.

[*To face page* 257.*]*

of the uncivilised natives of the Coast. There is not a tribe which would not, if circumstances permitted, act in precisely the same manner. We had evidence of this on our journey. Our carriers, composed of representatives of various tribes, exulting in the fact that Prempeh's power had been arrested, took advantage of opportunities to insult the unhappy monarch's people, who were peacefully engaged in bringing their produce to the Coast towns. We are justly proud of the thought that one of the chief characteristics of Englishmen is honesty. It necessarily follows that it is our duty to see justice meted out to the helpless, and to rescue the down-trodden. There may be differences of opinion as to details in policy in administering affairs in Her Majesty's Colonial possessions, but there cannot be a doubt that justice tempered with mercy is meted out to the very humblest negro subject in the Gold Coast Colony.

In his interesting *Historical Geography of West Africa*, Mr. C. P. Lucas of the Colonial Office, suggests the possibility of a discussion as to whether it is worth while for England to be hampered with a deadly climate, but adds: "There are other considerations, besides merely striking the balance of present and future advantages and disadvantages. The Africans have to be borne in mind as well as the English. It cannot seriously be doubted that of late years British rule has done something towards mitigating savagery, and introducing more human and more humane customs and modes of life. It is the case that the Christian religion has not made much progress yet; and quite possibly it will not make much progress for years to come, until generations grow up to whom fetish worship is a mere name. But the law and justice of a Christian people has its effect among West African nations, and the English would not be justified in withdrawing that law and justice, or in transferring to some other less qualified and less trained European nation the burden which history has given them to bear."

Our principal object in visiting Kumasi was the resuscitation of our work which had received a serious check some years previously. I have stated that the portion of land on which our old Mission house had formerly stood was claimed by the Government. It was, however, understood that we were to be compensated with a plot of land in a convenient part of the town. The Resident suggested that, as a certain amount of power had been vested in a committee composed of the chiefs of the town, it was desirable that I should see that committee. Accordingly, we waited upon the principal chief, who received us with the respectful salutation of "*Egya*" (father). We explained to him the object of our visit, viz., that we were anxious to again take up the work begun so long ago by Mr. Freeman, and for that purpose we desired a new plot of land. He cordially agreed with all that we said of the good feeling existing between the parent society and the people of Kumasi. The memory of the patriarch Freeman was venerated by all, and they would most gladly welcome us back again. But it was quite impossible for him to decide anything without first consulting his brother chiefs; he would, however, summon them to meet us the following morning at six o'clock.

We had resided in Africa much too long to imagine for one moment that the repeated and emphatic promises of punctuality would be fulfilled; but we were somewhat weary when, after waiting till half-past seven, we found that the matter could not then be discussed in consequence of the absence of some important members of the cabinet. Another hour passed, and then we were to be treated to a specimen of real Ashanti diplomacy. We stated our case : that our fathers in England were anxious to see the work resumed in Ashanti; we were the friends of all, the enemies of none; we earnestly desired to be made a blessing to their people. Our particular reason for meeting them that morning was to inform them that the Government had need of our old site; we were therefore driven to the necessity of looking for other suitable land. We had found a plot answering to our purpose; would they be pleased to grant it to us? The chiefs, with the linguist aforementioned—who, I am afraid, is not so benevolent as he appears—as their spokesman, informed us that our request came altogether as a surprise. Much as they desired to help us, it was quite beyond their power to make such a grant. The Government had taken their rights from them. In proof of their statement, they added that the Governor himself had already given a magnificent plot of land to the Basle Missionary Society. We pointed out that we had reason to believe that the Government was wishful to vest native chiefs with a certain amount of authority; it was wishful also to take counsel with them. They replied that if I would obtain the assurance of the Resident that such a gift as we desired was in their power to bestow, they would most readily grant it. I forthwith obtained the Resident's formal sanction. No sooner was this done than we were informed that the particular plot we desired could not be ours. But as it was known to be in their power to make grants of land, they very gladly gave us back our old land. It was a lovely idea, but we were quite at a loss to understand the meaning of the move. Was it that they wished us to throw obstacles in the way of the Royal proclamation relative to the open space? Or had they buried treasure on the site we had selected? We spent some time vainly endeavouring to reason with them. They gave half-a-dozen reasons for their inconsistent conduct. Eventually we decided to confer on the Government the privilege of settling the matter.

XIV DIFFICULTIES WITH OUR GOVERNMENT   261

It certainly is most perplexing that we should have experienced the slightest difficulty in settling this matter, especially in view of the fact that to the German Society, which had never previously owned an inch of land in the country, our generous Government gave a most magnificent site. Apart from this consideration, there was the fact that, in days gone by, our Society had spent thousands of pounds in Kumasi itself and had owned a plot of land in the central part of the town. So valuable was the site, that the Government claimed it for its own use. I am veiling nothing when I say that it was very right and proper for the Government to take our land, for I am a firm believer in the policy of the Government in Ashanti. But how it came to pass that the justice of our claim was so lightly regarded will ever remain a mystery. The oversight gave us considerable anxiety, and necessitated considerable correspondence. On July 4th—rather over four months later—Mr. Somerville was enabled to write: "We have overcome the difficulties of the chiefs, and this morning I have been with the linguist to the Resident and have settled everything, so that the land on the Nkoranza road is now ours in reality. The chiefs have granted it to us without cost. It certainly cannot be said that the Government has robbed the Ashantis for us, for the chiefs have given the land to us." It was of the greatest importance that no money should be paid for the land in question. For this would have denied the British Government the right of "doing justly," and it would also have established a bad precedent in dealing with the chiefs of other towns.

The three gentlemen who were associated with the present writer in the transference of that property have since passed away. Colonel Pigott died in England. Mr. G. E. Ferguson — a native Colonial officer, most highly esteemed by all who knew him—was killed while on an expedition with Lieutenant Henderson, and my colleague, Mr. Somerville, died within a month of penning the letter from which I have quoted the above extract.

Mr. Somerville had a wide circle of friends in Africa and in England. He was, as we have elsewhere shown, eminently qualified to fill the post to which he was first appointed—viz., the charge of our Gold Coast schools. He was very highly esteemed by his European and native colleagues, while the managers, teachers, and pupils of the schools he visited regarded him as a true friend.

In his anxiety to see the work in Ashanti permanently established, Mr. Somerville committed the fatal error of over-estimating and consequently over-taxing his strength. We had repeatedly urged him to take his furlough, to which he had so long been entitled, but our entreaties were vain. He recognised the mistake—as hundreds of his fellow-countrymen in that land have done—when it was too late.

Special mention must be made of the cheerful service rendered by Mr. Somerville to the Protestant soldiers of the West Yorkshire Regiment on their march to and from Kumasi. For as Canon Taylor Smith was attached to the Composite Battalion, and therefore had the care of the Nonconformists, so Somerville took the opportunity of ministering to the Anglicans of his company. And his services were greatly appreciated by members of the State Church as well as by the Free Churchmen. One instance of his unselfishness must be recorded; both on the march to Kumasi and on the return journey he was temporarily prostrated by fever, but he nevertheless very cheerfully handed over his hammock and carriers to a sick soldier. The kindly act was characteristic of our friend.

The last letter, dated Kumasi, July 12th, was received a fortnight after the cablegram announcing his death.

"The enclosed (medical certificate) speaks for itself. I have had another two days in bed—this makes the third attack in about six weeks. I rested for a fortnight after my last attack, but am none the better and, although it is to me the greatest disappointment, I must think about going home. I am, as MacCarthy says, suffering from weakness; in fact I feel worn out. Liver is bad, heart is weak, blood is thin, and nerves are shattered. And, as I promised both you and Mr. Hartley that I would not run undue risk, I am coming home. These four months in Ashanti, living and roughing it as I have had to do, have pulled me down so much that I do not feel confident of my own life if I stay.

"I can safely leave the work. Kumasi becomes emptier day by day. I am sending Baiden to Jabin, and will endeavour to get a teacher or two on the Coast when I go down.

"I do not expect to leave for a fortnight or three weeks, and as I am not seriously ill but "fagged out," I shall not cable from Cape Coast, but only cable my brother at Northwich from Grand Canary.

"You may be sure that I am more than disappointed."

Had Mr. Somerville left at once and gone direct to Cape Coast the result *might* have been otherwise. We cannot say. But we know that he turned aside to Bekwai to give final directions respecting the work, and that another attack of fever came on, and then came the weary, tiresome journey to the Coast, occupying some nine days. The hammock-men tell us that he fainted three times on the way. He battled bravely with a most virulent attack for a week at Cape Coast, and passed away on August the 2nd.

The work thus begun at the expense of his life at Kumasi, Bekwai, Abodom, Jabin, Mampon and Nsuta is being carried on by Rev. T. Morris, who was transferred from Accra. The growth of the Ashanti Mission will be watched with great interest. We long to see our Missionaries pushing their way into the far interior.

CHAPTER XV

THE LAST VOYAGE TO THE COAST, IN COMPANY WITH KINDRED SPIRITS—A BRIEF SUMMARY OF MISSION WORK, AND REFERENCES TO THREE "MISSIONARY-MADE MEN"

A REFERENCE to another furlough suggests most naturally that a considerable portion of time is spent away from the Coast recruiting health. I once met a gentleman in Africa who informed me that he had had eighteen years on the Coast, but he omitted to say that rather more than two-thirds of the time had been spent in England. The proportion of time occupied in furloughs is rarely as serious as that just mentioned. Government officers are required to complete twelve months' service on the Coast before being entitled to six months' leave of absence. The English employés of merchants have to complete two years, occasionally more, for a similar period of leave; but then it is said that out of every three men entering the latter service one dies. This statement I merely repeat; I am not in a position either to accept or reject it.

As a matter of fact, I had succeeded in completing seven years on the Coast, and my wife had completed three years before taking her second and final leave. For myself there was to be a short return to the old scenes. Matters requiring personal attention took me back again at the end of a busy furlough; the Missionary's furlough is usually crowded with work. On more than one occasion I have looked forward to the three weeks' voyage out, so as to secure at least a little rest before again taking up the work. This experience is shared by all Missionaries; and yet no one ought to complain, for all are at liberty to decline this extra work. Usually the Missionary is very thankful to find friends so interested in receiving the latest information, and the kindness shown by these in various parts of the country more than compensates for any little trouble one may have experienced.

In the first chapter I promised an account of a voyage. I now find that my book is larger than I anticipated, so that I must be brief. The last voyage out was made exceedingly agreeable by the fact that we had a steady ship, though a somewhat rough sea. The good ship *Bonny*, with Captain Windham, "went like a duck" (I think that that is a nautical expression). We had also a remarkably steady company of saloon passengers. Divinity was very much in evidence. Presbyterianism was represented by a minister who was taking a trip with his wife to the Islands. The Reverends Baylis, Humphreys and Cox (the last-named died after only a few months' residence in

Free Town), bound for Sierra Leone, represented the Anglican Church; there was also a Roman Catholic Missionary, as well as the present writer. The first week of January was observed by the evangelical ministers as is done in England. Meetings during the week were held in one of the cabins, so as not to obtrude upon the rest of the passengers. At the saloon services "Shibboleths" were carefully avoided, so that none of the passengers could gather which of the Missionaries represented the State and which the Free Church. "Not so much as one said that aught of the things which he had was his own; but we had all things in common." My Anglican friends and I, having so much mutual interest in West Africa, frequently took counsel, and, I believe, were alike refreshed.

At Sierra Leone half a dozen passengers left us; but we received the Reverend C. R. Johnson, a Wesleyan Missionary, who for a few years is representing the British and Foreign Bible Society in a district extending from Bathurst to the Niger delta. I have elsewhere stated our obligations to the Bible Society. These obligations are equally shared by the Church Missionary Society and by the Basle Mission Society. It is not too much to say that neither of these would be able to do its work without the invaluable aid of the greatest of all missionary societies.

At the Synod we had the pleasure of welcoming the Reverends Hinchcliff and Glandfield, who had recently arrived from England to take their part in the consolidation and extension of the Gold Coast Mission.

The reports that came in from the various circuits of the district were quite as encouraging as any that had been received during my connection with the Mission. But as extracts of previous reports have been made, I need not occupy any further space with information of this character.

It may perhaps be useful to take a retrospective glance at the growth of the Mission during the years 1887-96. The Mission sphere had extended north, west and east. The Atlantic limited our operations in the southern direction. Our chapels—some of them, indeed, inexpensive bamboo buildings, others quite costly and handsome—had increased in number from 56 to 111. Every expense incurred in these buildings had been met by native funds. The open-air centres for evangelistic work had trebled in number. European Missionaries increased from 2 to 4; natives from 14 to 23; catechists and day-school teachers from 84 to 263; Church members from 5,610 to 7,664; junior members from 1,136 to 5,410; catechumens from 557 to 3,387; Sunday scholars from 1,760 to 11,984; day scholars from 1,505 to 5,743. The ordinary annual district income had increased as follows: Weekly collections and contributions, £1,106 to £1,506; special contributions, from £1,107 to £1,561; seat rents (church), from £91 to £119; church and school buildings, from £245 to £1,063. Day-schools income from £353 to £2,560. The latter includes a Government grant in aid of education amounting to £1,500. This annual grant had grown from £200 in the nine years. I observe in one instance a decrease, viz., under the heading of "Sundries, Poor Fund," &c., £345 to £193. I must suppose that more than one fund—as the heading indicates—is represented here. For very great care was taken that the poor should not suffer, and, just as in our churches in England, lay stewards are severally appointed to the care of the circuit, the society, and the material buildings, so are there special appointments to minister to the necessitous poor. The collection taken at the Sacrament of the Lord's Supper is specially devoted to this purpose. It may here be mentioned that at a meeting at Kormantine, in 1896, four candidates desired Church membership; and ninety-two heathen, headed by a Fetish priest, came forward and voluntarily gave threepence each towards our "Poor Fund." To return to our retrospect, it will be seen that the ordinary annual district income had doubled in the period under review, *i.e.*, from £3,500 to £7,000.

In recording this progress mention must be made, not only of the paid native staff, but of the great force of lay preachers and Sunday School teachers, who ungrudgingly give their time to the great work. We could wish for some of our unpaid workers and, indeed, for some of our catechists and day school teachers, a more thorough equipment for the work. But we have the assurance that, "if there be first a ready mind, a man is accepted according to what he hath, not according to what he hath not."

On the homeward voyage a Government officer informed me that out of fifty Europeans who were at Cape Coast two years previously, only five were alive that day, which statement reminded me of the fact that an officer connected with the Ashanti expedition was informed that out of twenty who dined at the house of a British merchant on Christmas Day, 1894, only two were alive on the following Christmas Day. These statements appear incredible, and I am not in a position to testify to their accuracy, for one loses count of deaths as one loses count of attacks of fever; but with my knowledge of the treacherous climate, and particularly during the unusually trying period named, I should certainly not feel justified in questioning the statements. I can only express the hope that the residents at the Gold Coast may never again experience such a season.

Before quitting the Gold Coast I should like to introduce to my readers three friends with whom I have been associated during the whole of my connection with the Colony. Christian character grows but slowly, our converts are child-like and imperfect; but I may be permitted to say that, although I have known these gentlemen most intimately, I have never heard the faintest breath of suspicion by the most severe hypercritic.

The Rev. Jacob Anaman, F.R.G.S., entered our Gold Coast ministry in 1890. He had previously rendered good service to the Mission in many ways. I think I am right in saying that, from the time he passed out of our schools as a scholar until he came up as a candidate for our ministry, he was constantly engaged in imparting instruction either as a teacher or a translator. His contributions to and assistance in various vernacular publications have been very valuable. The Fanti reading book, prepared at the special request of the Cape Coast Sunday School teachers, has had a most appreciative circulation.

At his examination before the Synod of 1890, Mr. Anaman was warmly commended by the chairman, Mr. Halligey, for the care bestowed in the preparation. Subsequent examinations[1] have been most satisfactory. The whole of his probation—a period of four years—was spent at Cape Coast, where he greatly endeared himself, particularly among the young people upon whom he exercised a good influence. The Singing Band, composed of a large number of young people, which visits different parts of the circuit for the purpose of con-

---

[1] Although Mr. Anaman had only the plainest education of our Mission school, his text-books during the last year of probation were Salmon's *Introduction to the New Testament*, Rigg's *Church Organisation*, Findlay's *Epistles of St. Paul*, Smyth's *Old Documents*, the Book of Job and Second Epistle to the Corinthians, with the "Cambridge Bible for Schools" commentary. A "good" average mark was given, which was greatly to the probationer's credit, as he had important vernacular translation work on hand in addition to his by no means light pastoral duties.

ducting religious services, was organised by him and has been made a blessing to avowed heathen as well as to the Christians.

It may be of interest to know that, at the special request of His Excellency, Governor Sir Brandford Griffith, Mr. Anaman acted as interpreter during the interview with the Ashanti ambassadors in Cape Coast, December, 1894. His Excellency was anxious that the views of Prempeh's representatives should be faithfully and impartially stated.

Mr. Anaman is now in charge of a most important circuit in the district. At Salt Pond his services are greatly appreciated by both European and native residents.

A fellow countryman called on me one day and said: "I have just had occasion to look in on your friend Macfoy. I found him sitting in his little store reading the Bible." I replied, "I can quite believe that Joseph was thus employed; but I'll tell you what you never have seen in him—you have never seen a shady or dishonourable action in his business or private life. I don't mind challenging you!" The friend admitted that Macfoy would "pass muster."

In reply to inquiries Mr. Macfoy informed me that he was born at Fernando Po in 1831, when the island was a British possession. Shortly afterwards, on the transfer of the island to Spain, he, with his parents and other re-captives, were removed

A Collection of Curiosities.

1. Tom-toms.
2. Stools—cut from solid blocks.
3. Chair, seat formed of Sheepskin.
4. Top of Skull used as Wine Cup at Heathen Festival (see p. 167).
5. Soup Dish from Bekwai.
6. Skull from Kumasi (see p. 255).
7. War horn, small Elephant's Tusk covered with Crocodile Skin and graced with six Human Jaw Bones, representing three Wars.
8. Musical Instruments.
9. State Sword, Handle of Wood, covered with thin Gold Plate.
10. Housewife's Colander.
11. Carved Gourd.
12. Wooden Sandals.
13. Bush Hat.
14. Skin of Python (see p. 121), measures twelve feet, six inches.
15. Sportsman's Hunting Belt.

to Sierra Leone. Very speedily the head of the family died, and the lad found a home at the European Mission House. He was thus brought into contact with English Missionaries, whose names are to-day remembered with affection at Sierra Leone. He was greatly impressed by an exhortation from a dying Missionary to give himself entirely to the service of Christ. Several years of apparent indifference followed, but the entreaty was ever with him, and when quite a young man he decided, by the help of God, to live an out-and-out Christian life.

I would that I knew more of the subsequent career of Mr. Macfoy up to the period at which I first met him. I am quite convinced that during the years that found him moving about in different parts of the Coast honourably engaged in trade, he commanded the respect of all with whom he came into contact; for, in his house of business at Cape Coast, and as a member of the Local Chamber of Commerce, he was regarded by Europeans and natives alike as a thoroughly capable business man, and by his irreproachable character he became "a living epistle, known and read of all men."

As a member of the Church we found him most consistent, and his knowledge of the Word of God, which he greatly loved, was most helpful to the members of the classes that met in the Mission House during my early residence there. Our West Indian, "declared Wesleyan," soldiers found in him a true friend and counsellor. I feel I ought to add that he recognised that his comparative prosperity in his unpretentious little business house was due, humanly speaking, to the blessings of the Missionary Society; and his gifts to the Mission have been both munificent and unostentatious. He had a perfect abhorrence of all shams and anything that savoured of display.

I have written in the past tense, for Mr. Macfoy, on retiring from business, has, with his good wife, left Cape Coast, and has returned to Sierra Leone to spend the eventide of life among his own people. It need hardly be said that he continues to take an active interest in the welfare of his loved Church. I am sure that my readers will join me in wishing that heaven's choicest blessing may continue to rest upon the household of one whom we may regard as one of "God's untitled noblemen."

My last reference is to the senior native minister of our Gold Coast Mission. The Rev. James A. Solomon is eighty years of age; he was born at Accra in 1818. It was with great difficulty that I succeeded in getting my information from the "old man," as, after the custom of the country, we reverently call him; for he shrinks from publicity.

Mr. Solomon recognises, as all converted men do, that there is a vast difference between the mere profession of Christianity and the transformation of the heart and life. In his case the first took place some eight or nine years before the second. To use Scripture language he had the "form of godliness," but knew nothing experimentally of its "power." If this distinction were more generally understood we should not have to mourn over the "missionary failure" in the lives of individuals.

After a brief visit to England, Mr. Solomon had the privilege of accompanying the Rev. T. B. Freeman in 1841 to Kumasi, when the Committee's present of a carriage[1] for King Kweku Duah was conveyed thither. It was the wish of the Missionaries of those days that Mr. Solomon should have the benefit of special training at the Theological Institution, but the frequent deaths in the European staff rendered such a course impossible, and so, as a catechist, he was engaged for eight years in various parts of the Colony, leading pagans from their gross sins to acknowledge God as their Lord.

It is not surprising that the members of the Church, recognising that he was moved to the work of the ministry, unanimously recommended him to the Conference as a candidate. In 1853, at Abakrampa, Mr. Solomon entered upon his probation. For thirty-one years he was "separated" to the active work of the ministry, during which period he was engaged at Anamabu, Accra, Dominasi, Dix Cove, Tacquah, and Winnebah, in most useful service. In 1884, after forty-three years' employment by the Mission, our old friend retired, and is now enjoying his well-earned rest at Cape Coast, although gladly lending assistance to other active workers.

[1] It may be mentioned that the carriage was submitted to Her Majesty the Queen and H.R.H. the Prince Consort, who took a great interest in this visit to Ashanti.

Mr. Solomon has known great sorrows. Six of his nine children, with their mother, have been taken from him. Two of his sons were lost by drowning; two daughters were taken only a few years since. It has always been a very real pleasure to meet the veteran, wearing the white flower of a blameless life, and to hear him relate the triumphs of the Gospel, and the deliverance of thousands of his fellow-countrymen from the bondage in which they were once held.

I have instanced these three friends as "Missionary-made men." I might have added to their number. Although, personally, I have had little to do with their advance in the Christian life, for the youngest was a Christian long before I had dreamed of going to Africa, yet I have the consciousness that there are other cases in which I have been used in the development of the Christian characters. And concerning these one can gratefully write, "You that were sometime alienated and enemies in your mind, by wicked works, yet now hath He reconciled. In the body of His flesh through death, to present you holy and unblameable and unreprovable in His sight. If ye continue in the faith grounded and settled, and be not moved away from the hope of the Gospel, which ye have heard, and which was preached to every creature which is under heaven."

www.ingramcontent.com/pod-product-compliance
Lightning Source LLC
Chambersburg PA
CBHW031851220426
43663CB00006B/573